60 0600408 3

TELEPEN

AF748962

Bath University Library

Author ....

Title ....

....

Book No ....

This book should be returned not later than the last date stamped below. The period of loan may be extended on request if no other reader wishes to use the book. Books may not be renewed by telephone.

NOT FOR LOAN UNTIL 13 SEP 1984

12 OCT 1984

CANCELLED

I.L.L 12.8.85

CANCELLED

U4 60940

19 FEB 1990

6 DEC 90

CANCELLED

19 DEC 2001

INEQUALISING TRADE?

A Study of Traditional North/South Specialisation in the context of Terms of Trade Concepts

INEQUALISING TRADE?

A Study of Traditional North/South Specialisation in the Context of Terms of Trade Concepts

JOHN SPRAOS

CLARENDON PRESS · OXFORD
in co-operation with the
UNITED NATIONS CONFERENCE ON TRADE AND DEVELOPMENT
1983

Oxford University Press, Walton Street, Oxford OX2 6DP

London Glasgow New York Toronto
Delhi Bombay Calcutta Madras Karachi
Kuala Lumpur Singapore Hong Kong Tokyo
Nairobi Dar es Salaam Cape Town
Melbourne Auckland

and associated companies in
Beirut Berlin Ibadan Mexico City Nicosia

Oxford is a trade mark of Oxford University Press

Published in the United States
by Oxford University Press, New York

© United Nations 1983

All rights reserved. No part of this publication may be reproduced, stored in a retrieval system, or transmitted, in any form or by any means, electronic, mechanical, photocopying, recording, or otherwise, without the prior permission of Oxford University Press

British Library Cataloguing in Publication Data

Spraos, John
Inequalising trade?
I. Commerce
I. Title
380.1 HF1007
ISBN 0-19-828458-6

Library of Congress Cataloging in Publication Data

Spraos, John.
Inequalising trade?
Bibliography: p.
Includes index.
1. International economic relations. I. United Nations. II. Title.
HF1411.S7 1983 382'.091722-01724 83-3996
ISBN 0-19-828458-6

UNIVERSITY OF BATH LIBRARY
15 FEB 2024
Withdrawn

Typeset by Joshua Associates, Oxford
and printed in Great Britain
at the University Press, Oxford
by Eric Buckley
Printer to the University

UNIVERSITY OF BATH LIBRARY
11 18 JUL 1984
330.3

PREFACE

When I proposed this project to the United Nations Conference on Trade and Development (UNCTAD) during my period of consultancy in 1974-5 I did not anticipate that it would take eight years to the time it appeared in print. Two spells as head of my Department and a variety of extraneous preoccupations are partly responsible, but the prolonged search for data which in the end could not be found or were deemed unusable and a slow process of intellectual self-development are mainly to blame.

The outcome is a mixture of the novel and the traditional which will, I hope, have a wide appeal but which will probably not be above controversy since the subject-matter lies at the core of North/South economic relations and has engaged the passions and partisanship of even staid academics.

Central to the book is the developing countries' deep-rooted and long-standing concern with the structure of world trade and specialisation which they inherited in the years following World War II. This concern has either been arrogantly dismissed as inconsistent with economic theory or sympathetically acknowledged but mostly without effective theoretical and empirical underpinning. For the sympathetically inclined there is here a major challenge which needs to be met and this book makes an attempt at meeting it. In doing so, it eschews the easy, but in the long run not necessarily convincing, appeal to the hardship which has been inflicted on the South in the early 1980s by the North's deep recession. Instead, it seeks its empirical underpinning in the preceding two decades which were, for the greater part, expansionary.

The book is addressed to professional economists and students of economics, but in the widest sense of these terms because the contents are not technically demanding by present-day standards and also because with the aid of the first chapter the drift of the argument can be followed while skimming over some of the tedious technical detail.

Hopefully, via the economists, wider world opinion formers, policy makers and decision takers in both North and South can be reached since the light thrown on the topics treated here bears materially on their perceptions of issues of major international significance.

To place the book in chronological perspective it should be said that a last major redraft was undertaken in 1980. Some modifications were then made in the summer of 1981, after which only a few relevant bibliographical additions were inserted.

Over eight years I have accumulated many intellectual debts, so many that the list of creditors would fill a page of a telephone directory. I will not list them individually, but collectively I thank warmly my colleagues at UNCTAD for the help they gave me during and after the year I spent there and my colleagues at University College London on whose expertise I have drawn more than they realise. Exceptionally, I mention first Geraldine Wegener, who toiled with me to collect, process, and interpret data which I ultimately decided, partly at her prompting, were too unrobust to serve as evidence—but for the latter, the book would have been longer and she would have been a named co-author of a chapter in it; second, Holly Sutherland who enhanced her already high reputation for dependability in dealing with a substantial share of the computations; and third, Malcolm Pemberton who, having read the manuscript from end to end with a care far exceeding the call of duty to a colleague, proffered advice on which I could instinctively rely.

I gladly share any merits of the book with my intellectual creditors but the errors are mine alone. While UNCTAD has sponsored this work, for which I am grateful, it has no responsibility for and must not be assumed to agree with any of its contents.

Chapters II and III are modified versions of papers which appeared in the *Greek Economic Review* and the *Economic Journal* respectively and thanks are due to their editors for permission to reprint.

University College
London

JOHN SPRAOS

CONTENTS

I

OVERVIEW

This chapter can serve as a summary of the material and as a travel guide to the territory covered in this book. To assist in the latter function the sequence of topics treated follows broadly that of the succeeding chapters. Each section heading is followed by a bracketed reference to the chapter to which the section contents relate, except where no one-to-one relation exists.

But primarily the intention is to offer at this early stage a broad based exposition of the leading ideas and empirical issues which underlie the monograph, to set out the framework into which the largely self-contained individual chapters fit and to highlight the theme which binds them together.

A less neutral language than in subsequent chapters is occasionally permitted to surface.

1. THE STARTING-POINT

The starting-point is that developing countries have been intensely dissatisfied with the traditional pattern of trade and specialisation which they inherited from the colonial period.

The context of this dissatisfaction is both the absolute poverty of the developing countries and their relative poverty *vis-à-vis* developed countries. The emphasis in this monograph is on relative poverty and the question which will be most insistently addressed is whether the traditional pattern of specialisation has contributed to the alleviation or aggravation of inequality.

2. SOME MEANINGS

'Traditional' here means the pattern whereby the developing countries specialise in and export primary commodities in return for manufactured imports from the developed countries. If petroleum is included, this remains the overwhelming pattern to the present day. If fuels are excluded, some three-fifths of developing country exports in the 1970s still consisted of commodities and the erosion of this pattern by growing manufactured exports has been heavily concentrated in only a handful of developing countries.

Fuels will in fact be excluded hereafter because, since the effective cartelisation of petroleum in 1973, they have ceased to be a source of grievance for the developing countries as a whole (though the net fuel importers among them have suffered). Despite this exclusion the traditional pattern still dominates and will be at the centre of our attention.

In empirical contexts the developing countries will be understood to comprise (where not otherwise stated) what the United Nations Secretariat refers to as the 'developing market economies' which are the large residual group after the 'developed market economies' and the 'centrally planned economies' are taken out. Exclude Europe, Canada, the United States, Soviet Asia and Mongolia, Japan and China, Australia and New Zealand, and South Africa and in the rest you almost have a good list of developing countries in the sense of this monograph.

Not all international agencies adhere to the same list and the UN Secretariat itself has made some changes over time. Cuba, Israel, Zimbabwe (formerly Rhodesia), Yugoslavia, Greece, Turkey, and the states of former French Indo-China are the major countries among those prone to be treated non-uniformly, but this is a minor irritant because in the broad sweep of these groupings their combined economic weight is small.

When the term developed countries is used in empirical contexts it will refer to the developed market economies. 'North/South' is a convenient shorthand expression for the developed/developing dichotomy and will be used frequently.

3. AGGREGATION AND DISAGGREATION

The developing countries are obviously not a homogeneous group and for many purposes it is desirable to disaggregate them. Yet in the context of this monograph it is of the essence that they be treated as a whole. The central concern relates to their combined position *vis-à-vis* developed countries and in this frame of reference fragmentation is not just unhelpful, it is a positive hindrance. The fallacy of composition must be guarded against much more than has been customary. To illustrate, if the expansion of tea-growing is good for Kenya, it cannot be concluded that it is good for the South as a whole, because Kenyan gains are at the cost of bigger losses by existing tea producers;

while it was good for South Korea or Taiwan to have export-oriented industrialisation it does not follow that all developing countries simultaneously should aim for export orientation, because they may be scoring gains against each other and/or triggering off more protectionist responses from the North.

In contrast, some disaggregation of commodities is called for at the empirical level. Whether they are exhaustible or reproducible, whether their production is or is not dominated by developing countries, and whether a high proportion of developing country output of a given commodity is or is not exported, affects very materially the outcome as viewed from the angle of inequality.

4. DIFFERENT PERCEPTIONS OF NORTH AND SOUTH

The dominant view in the North is that trade is equalising. This cannot rest on Samuelson's (1948, 1949) factor price equalisation theorem which is known to be unrobust, or on the weaker version of a 'tendency towards' equalisation which had been propounded earlier by Ohlin (1933), to which Samuelson (1971) eventually gravitated but which has been under a cloud of successive empirical findings, starting with Leontieff (1953), to the effect that the observed factor intensity of imports and exports is more often than not inconsistent with it.

Nor can it rest on the more robust theorem that some trade is better than no trade, because this does not say anything about the distribution of gains from trade.[1] Even more to the point, the no-trade alternative is not a benchmark with any practical relevance and cannot help in refuting or sustaining the grievances of the South. The empirically meaningful question and the one which this monograph principally addresses is whether the pattern of trade and specialisation is *incrementally* inequalising, i.e. inequalising relatively to an identifiable earlier point in time. There is no theorem in the orthodox canon which denies this—there could not be, since the theoretically admitted case of 'immiserizing growth' would have served as a counter-example—and therefore an affirmative answer to inequalisation, if this is what comes out, is not theoretically heterodox nor counter-intuitive, even if shocking to dominant faith.

The North's dominant view has had limited success in persuading minds in the South and no success at all in capturing hearts. The South's dissatisfaction with the traditional pattern of trade and specialisation remains firmly implanted.

This dissatisfaction has been conceptualised mainly along two lines so far: (a) a theory of deteriorating terms of trade over time; (b) a theory of unequal exchange at any point of time.

5. UNEQUAL EXCHANGE

Not much is said about (b) in this monograph. Only section 3(c) of Chapter II focuses directly on it and views it as a step towards 'dynamic unequal exchange'—a version of the unequal exchange hypothesis which shades into (a).

A severe critic of (b) would emphasise the penumbra of nonsense associated with some unequal exchange thinkers, such as the notion that, except for frictional and transitory difficulties, an increase of wages in the South to a level that would equalise them with the North's is viable if only it could be engineered.

A sympathetic but patronising view would accept the validity of egalitarian values in unequal exchange thinking—exchange is said to be unequal if associated with unequal wages—but would question whether they yield any analytical insights or policy guidelines.

Somebody seeking to distil the element of good sense would acknowledge that unequal exchange thinkers operate and seek answers in a critical area which orthodox theory has left in a vacuum. As noted already, orthodox theory does not say how the gains from trade are distributed among trading partners. This does not mean it does not indulge in taxonomic exercises of the 'if this, then that' variety. But it does mean that it is agnostic about the force or forces that may dominate the outcome. To seek to fill this vacuum is not just legitimate, it is desirable. That this is what at least some unequal exchange theorists are trying to do emerges most clearly in the work of Mitra (1977, appendix to Chapter 3, Chapter 7) and in the later writings of Emmanuel whose book *Unequal Exchange* (1972) initiated the whole idea.

The core of what they, and some less heterodox writers such as Helleiner (1980, Chapter 2), are saying is that in a world where, unlike the perfect competition model, market power matters, those who have more of it gain most from trade—and may gain more than the global gain accruing from trade, at the expense of the partner's impoverishment, once the partner is locked-in in a certain specialisation.[2] In Emmanuel's case this is particularised to the market power exercised by labour unions in the North, which is said to have raised real wages at the expense of living standards in the South.

In this minimalist form the unequal exchange hypothesis cannot be summarily dismissed, yet it will be laid aside for the pragmatic reason that to test it and assess its significance one has to resort to the methodology of the 'counter-factual'—conjuring, for purposes of comparison, a situation wherein all market power is absent—which is unconvincing.[3]

6. DETERIORATING TERMS OF TRADE: THEORY (Chapter II)

The history of (a) above—deteriorating terms of trade—goes back to the early post-World War II years. Prebisch (1950) and Singer (1950), almost simultaneously but independently, launched this hypothesis on to a remarkably influential course. The ideas associated with it provided the momentum for the creation of UNCTAD with Prebisch himself as its first Secretary General.

The theory started on a very strong but false note. It was strong because the contrasting market structures for commodities and manufactures—a competitive structure in commodities, translating increases in productivity into lower prices, and a monopolistic structure in manufactures, causing increases in productivity to be matched by increases in money wages—were supposed to lead to the deterioration result unambiguously, admitting no exceptions or qualifications. It was false, however, because it was inconsistent with market clearing for primary commodities, a feature which cannot be reconciled with Prebisch's assumption of competitive conditions for commodities.

Perhaps because of its strong implications, this fallacious argument is the one which became most closely associated with the name of Prebisch, which is not only unfortunate but also unfair because soon afterwards Prebisch introduced other considerations which can be validly adduced as pushing towards deterioration, in particular income-inelastic demand for commodities and pressure of excess labour in the South. Both of these have strong empirical support and subsequently gained prominence in the literature, the former via a rapid succession of papers on the terms of trade which followed Hicks's 'Inaugural Lecture' (1953) and the latter via Lewis's (1953) striking special case of 'unlimited supplies of labour'.

However, these valid considerations do not exert (except in special cases) complete dominance over all other factors, so that the theoretical signpost which points towards terms of trade deterioration in the South's traditional trade is not free from ambiguity. Thus the empirical evidence on this issue becomes critical.

7. DETERIORATING TERMS OF TRADE: EVIDENCE (Chapter III)

As a 'man of affairs' Prebisch appreciated the need for empirical support and found it in data which the UN Secretariat was putting into circulation at that time. The writers who tried to impugn Prebisch's conclusion that the evidence over the period 1870–1938 was consistent with the deterioration hypothesis are legion; they adduced conceptual, practical, and statistical considerations, but they may be fairly judged to have completely failed. Those who seek material for the thesis that partisanship, conscious or subconscious, prevails over academic detachment could find support in this episode. But where intellectual onslaught failed, developments which occurred with the passage of time succeeded.

When the data base is extended to include the period since World War II, the consistency of the deterioration hypothesis with the evidence is open to doubt. Ironically, this is despite the fact that the terms of trade data since 1950, when viewed on their own, show a marked deterioration. As the deterioration was heavily concentrated in the late fifties, the Prebisch-Singer thesis was given a very strong empirical boost. But misleadingly so, because the early fifties were a very exceptional peak and because when the post-1950 period is viewed as a whole it can be seen to offset the deterioration which had previously dominated.

Of course long-run statistics are fragile, they are subject to theoretical, practical, and methodological reservations and are rarely tailor-made for testing a particular hypothesis. So in a perfectionist sense we shall never be entirely sure, but a strong negative terms of trade trend must be discounted.

At a more basic level, the one-dimensional nature of the terms of trade criterion gives rise to reservations. If a terms of trade change were exogenous, it would normally be possible to identify it with a gain/loss of welfare, be it absolute or relative to the trading partners. If a change is endogenous, its welfare significance is not obvious.

History offers examples of drastic terms of trade deterioration which were an integral part of and occurred at a time when there was, or the foundations were being laid for, a great economic expansion relatively to the rest of the world. The deterioration of the United Kingdom's terms of trade in the second quarter of the nineteenth century is one example. Japan in the inter-war years provides another.

Other illustrations of the theme that the terms of trade are liable to be a misleading criterion can be drawn from a wide variety of circumstances. Nurkse (1959), in a well-known work in which he examined the relation between the world trade system and underdevelopment, chanced to pick on the period 1928–57 at the end of which the terms of trade of primary products were almost certainly no worse than at the beginning. He did not dwell on this, but argued instead that the developing countries were severely handicapped by the system, as evidenced by the fact that the volume of their exports (excluding petroleum) had grown much more slowly than that of developed countries. He could not have observed anything worrying had he focused on the terms of trade.

Baumol's (1965) analysis of the seemingly unrelated problem of the performing arts is apt also. As productivity in the performing arts grew more slowly than in other sectors, but wages had to keep in step, the relative price of the former had to rise continuously. This improvement of the terms of trade of the performing arts did not cause him much pleasure: he worried that they would price themselves out of the market and that the number of performing artists would shrink.[4]

The point of these illustrations is the obvious one that terms of trade changes usually come as part of a package and that a deterioration or improvement in the terms of trade can be the inevitable consequence of other developments which may make the net outcome in welfare terms ambiguous. There may be no grief in the deterioration of the terms of trade if it is the result of rapid increases in productivity or (in the context of unemployment) in job opportunities.

In sum, it is unfortunate that the developing countries became ideologically locked into an unsuitable one-dimensional concept and one which, in retrospect, did not exhibit the statistical trend predicted for it.

8. FACTORIAL TERMS OF TRADE AND RELATIVE WELFARE (Chapter IV)

But this is not so much a conclusion as a challenge; a challenge to do better, to try to conceptualise in a superior way the dissatisfaction of the developing countries with the traditional pattern of trade and specialisation and to cover the conceptual bones with empirical flesh.

We are interested in relative living standards. If we take this to mean, as we shall, the relative size of average consumption baskets in two economies, then it is an identity that, with constant populations, balanced trade, and a constant share of investment in output, the movement in relative living standards can be exhaustively decomposed into employment, productivity, and terms of trade changes.

The terms of trade is thus only one of the three dimensions which are relevant. But we are not focusing on entire economies, only on those sectors which are most closely associated with the traditional pattern of North/South trade: the manufacturing sector in the North; the commodity-producing sector in the South. This deliberate narrowing of vision means that all three dimensions cannot be mechanically transferred to the problem in hand and that the results obtained must be tempered by general equilibrium considerations which inevitably slip out of the restricted range of vision. This applies in particular to the employment dimension.

But at first keep employment out of the problem by assuming constant participation rates and full employment in both economies. We are left with productivity and the terms of trade. These two dimensions are combined in the long-standing concept of the double factorial terms of trade (DFTT) which is defined as

$$\text{DFTT} \equiv P \frac{\Pi_c}{\Pi_m^*}.$$

Π signifies output per person employed (productivity), the subscripts c and m refer to commodity production and manufacturing respectively while the asterisk distinguishes symbols appertaining to the North from (non-asterisked) symbols appertaining to the South. P is the ratio of two price indices, P_c which is the price index of the South's commodities and P_m which is the index of the North's manufactures. P is thus the terms of trade which will be referred to hereafter in an abbreviated form as NBTT (net barter terms of trade) to avoid confusing them with other terms of trade concepts such as DFTT.

In using the DFTT concept this monograph can appeal to a long tradition as well as to current interest in the concept. As many authors have observed—Viner (1937, p. 561), Baldwin (1955), Morgan (1963)—the classical economists viewed the DFTT as the most important of the terms of trade concepts. Others who shared the classical view include Haberler (1936, p. 162) and Robertson (1952, p. 175). Emmanuel's (1972) unequal exchange hypothesis borders on DFTT territory while Amin (1976) opines expicitly that his version of unequal exchange could be tested by reference to DFTT time series. Prebisch did not directly avail himself of the DFTT concept, but in his thinking the productivity dimension had as much prominence as the NBTT dimension, so, unsurprisingly, Rodriguez (1977) writing under the editorship of Prebisch felt that a valid test of Prebisch's hypothesis of terms of trade deterioration had to be sought in the behaviour of the DFTT. Lewis (1969) placed the DFTT at the core of his Wicksell lectures, while others, e.g. Griffin (1974) and Streeten (1982), have incorporated in varying degrees the DFTT in their analyses.

In Chapter IV it is shown that the DFTT, by assigning equal weights to relative price and relative productivity, provide an accurate measure of changes in the relative size of consumption baskets only in special cases. One of these is when the fraction of income devoted to tradable goods should be apportioned in the same way by consumers in both trading countries, for example if in the North the share of home exportables is x, then in the South the share of imports should also be x. The other obtains when the relative price component of the DFTT is trendless. As these are cases which are closely enough matched in the North/South context for the period for which data can be assembled, the simplicity of the DFTT and the weight of tradition behind it will be deemed to compensate for a lack of generality.

There is, however, at the empirical level a major snag: employment data which are needed to compute Π_c are not available.

It turns out, though, that this difficulty can be circumvented at the same time as a third dimension—the employment dimension—is integrated in our index of inequalisation.

The need for and the implementation of such integration differs according as we deal with a typically fully employed economy or an economy suffering from chronic unemployment. Recall that we are focusing on the traditional exportables-producing sectors. If there is full employment and high mobility between occupations, the gain of price-weighted output from employing one more person in exportables is approximately offset by the loss of employing one person less in other sectors. If, on the other hand, the extra person in exportables was previously unemployed, the opportunity cost is zero and the increase of employment in exportables raises the combined output of all sectors just as much as a rise in productivity and must be given the same weight as the latter.

These are polar cases. But, while mindful of the possible bias, it is convenient for empirical estimation to operate as if the polar cases did apply: full employment in the North and unemployment in the

South. For all but the last three or four years of the period 1960–78 for which data can be assembled, the North had something approaching full employment while the South was subject to chronic unemployment throughout. And it hardly needs adding that many models feature this as one of the most fundamental asymmetries across the developed/developing divide.

The implication for the inequalisation index is of course asymmetric. Employment in the South's exportables-producing sector is relevant but in the North's it is not. So that

$$\text{employment-corrected DFTT or ECDFTT} \equiv \frac{P\Pi_c N_c}{\Pi_m^*},$$

where N_c is an index of employment in the South's traditional exportables. Recalling that $P \equiv P_c/P_m$,

$$\text{ECDFTT} \equiv \frac{V}{P_m \Pi_m^*},$$

where $V \equiv P_c \Pi_c N_c \equiv$ index of output of exportables valued at current prices.

This kills two birds with one stone. It extends the inequalisation index to comprise all three dimensions—employment as well as relative price and relative productivity—and it loses the empirically troublesome Π_c.

If this index declines, inequality across the North/South divide increases and vice versa. But remember we are focusing on the sectors producing traditional exportables. The index cannot and is not intended to say anything about equalisation or inequalisation across the board, only about the contribution of the sectors moulded by the traditional pattern of specialisation.

A complication arises if exhaustible resources are traded against reproducible goods, but of this more later.

9. MODELLING THE MOVEMENT OF FACTORIAL TERMS OF TRADE
(Chapter V)

At this point we could proceed straight to the empirical evidence. But it is instructive to pause for a little theorising.

If two hypothetical countries, Northland and Southland, were fully specialised economies, exporting reproducible goods but neither making close substitutes for what the other exports, an almost unambiguous conclusion of ECDFTT deterioration for Southland could be established, in the context of a market-clearing model, from three assumptions about Southland exportables. Two of these—income and price-inelastic demand—apply with overwhelming empirical support to the traditional exportables of developing countries. The third, valid for many such exportables, is that a high proportion of output is exported.

The basic reasoning is elementary. If the outputs of M^* (manufactures) and of C (commodities), which are the respective countries' exportables, increase proportionately, the relative price of C will fall because the demand for it is income inelastic. Thus the P component of the ECDFTT will deteriorate. If C output grows at a slower rate than M^* output, the P component need not deteriorate and may improve but the slower growth of C will be due either to slower productivity growth in C- than M^*-making, in which case the Π_c/Π_m^* component of the ECDFTT will deteriorate, or to more unemployment in Southland, in which case the N_c component of the ECDFTT will decline. While an improvement in the P component which more than compensates for the deterioration of Π_c/Π_m^* and N_c cannot be ruled out, it can be heavily discounted. If, alternatively, C output grows faster than M^* output, the underlying productivity and/or employment increases in Southland will be unambiguously more than offset by a deterioration of the P component because of the price inelasticity of demand for C.

There are three points most worth retaining from this simple theorising. The first is that a hypothesis of inequalising specialisation (incrementally inequalising, to be more precise) can be solidly founded on income and price inelasticity, than which there cannot be anything more commonplace or more strongly backed by empirical evidence in the context of developing countries.

The second, which is only implicit in the above exposition, is that under the stated assumptions incremental inequalisation is not only consistent with constancy of relative price, it is inevitable. This is of some importance if a hypothesis of inequalisation is to be sustainable against the background of apparently trendless NBTT in the traditional trade of developing countries. The third point is that Southland cannot avoid the inequalisation trend by improving its record of productivity growth. For with price-inelastic demand this will be more than offset by the deterioration of the P component of the ECDFTT.

Two further important points can be made by relaxing two assumptions which have been embedded in the theoretical reasoning.

First, let Southland export some exhaustible resources in return for reproducible goods. There is now, built-in, a factor which tends to push upwards Southland's NBTT since the pure royalty element in the price of exhaustible resources must rise at a rate no smaller than the real interest rate on alternative assets if the resource owners are not to have an incentive to extract and market the entire stock of reserves very quickly in order to acquire other assets with the proceeds. Thus the *P* component will now cause the ECDFTT index to move less negatively or even positively. But note that by the same token a constant ECDFTT index no longer represents distributional constancy between Northland and Southland, for Southland is not being compensated for resource depletion; it is, in effect, consuming its mineral capital without a matching increase in other assets.

Distributional constancy now requires that the ECDFTT index be rising. If the reserves of natural resources are vast, likely to last many hundreds of years at current and prospective rates of depletion, the rate of ECDFTT increase needed for distributional constancy is very small. But nevertheless the perspective in which one views the behaviour of the index is affected because in the developed/developing context the movement of natural resources is predominantly one way. In any event, the need for commodity disaggregation in the empirical side of this work becomes apparent: exhaustible resources must be treated separately.

Second, drop complete specialisation. When Northland produces some of the commodities that Southland does, or close substitutes for them, the increment of output in Southland generated by growth of either productivity or employment could displace Northland production of the corresponding commodities and have repercussions on relative prices less adverse than before.

This is the principal mechanism by which the ECDFTT index may be prevented from deteriorating or helped to improve. The practical importance of this mechanism depends *inter alia* on what proportion of Southland exportables do face Northland-produced substitutes, what is the share of Northland production in such commodities and, if the share is substantial, whether a protectionist reaction is triggered off.

In the developed/developing context coffee illustrates a traditional exportable that has no close substitute produced in the developed world, cotton one which has, but faces no protection (except when incorporated in textiles), and sugar one which has and faces stiff protection. Some further disaggregation by commodity to take into account the most important of these considerations is again called for in the empirical work.

Obviously then the theory does not lead to a firm prediction about the direction of the ECDFTT; a balance of forces is involved. This is not the same thing as saying that we must turn to the empirical evidence with a blank mind. More than a quarter of all non-fuel primary exports of developing to developed countries consists of goods which have no substitutes produced in any significant quantities in developed countries. These exert a one-way pull on the ECDFTT. The remaining three-quarters are subject to mutually offsetting forces and if those pushing the ECDFTT upwards prevail, they would do so *on balance*. The probability that they would match the one-way pressure exerted in the other direction by the first quarter must be low, and all the more so if some allowance is made for protectionist responses by developed countries. The presumption must therefore be that the overall ECDFTT will deteriorate, that an incrementally inequalising trend will have the upper hand.

10. EVIDENCE (Chapter VI)

The V component of the ECDFTT formula, i.e. the value of output of non-fuel primary exportables of developing countries, can be proxied by the value of these exports. One may feel reasonably confident about this in the case of commodities of which a very high proportion is exported, which is the case for tropical beverages, natural rubber, most non-ferrous metals, etc. But for the rest such proxying would be open to doubt.

Alternatively, the value of output can be computed as the product of volume produced and export unit value. This too has its own problems and is laborious. It has been done for commodities which accounted for nearly half of total non-fuel primary exports of developing countries in 1970. The series obtained by the two methods are mutually supportive in the sense that they convey broadly the same message. So this half of the data may be viewed with some confidence. But data which relate to or incorporate the other half must obviously be treated with caution.

The data extend from 1960 to 1978. The initial date is determined by convenient availability. At the time of writing the terminal date could have been stretched to 1979 and very tentatively to 1980 by using provisional data. But this was unnecessary because trend-fitting has been confined to 1960-77 anyway. The reason for this is that in 1977 there was a very sharp peak in the NBTT of the developing countries' traditional trade, in consequence also a peak in their ECDFTT, and if the maintained hypothesis is that the ECDFTT deteriorate, it is proper to stiffen the test that it has to pass by truncating the data set at the last peak year.

An alternative truncation is made at the end of 1974. The state of more or less full employment which prevailed in the North up to 1974 came to an end. As the asymmetric treatment of employment in the ECDFTT formula depended on unemployment being a chronic feature in only one of the trading partners, the applicability of the formula beyond 1974 is open to question. It happens, however, that the alternative truncations do not give qualitatively divergent results, so in commenting on these results the two data spans will not be considered separately.

In keeping with the need for commodity disaggregation we can take first the minerals of developing countries and consider their ECDFTT *vis-à-vis* manufactures of developed countries. As near as no matter they are trendless. This does not necessarily mean, however, that they are distributionally neutral since, as we saw, trendlessness fails to compensate for depletion of resources. The share of minerals in non-fuel exports of developing countries was a little over a quarter in 1970.

Next take a group of six agricultural commodities: cocoa, coffee, cotton, rubber, sugar, and tea. They were selected because each has an important share in the South's export trade and because the South dominates the world exports of each of these commodities. In 1970 the six accounted for nearly a half of all developing country primary exports of agricultural origin.

Their ECDFTT *vis-à-vis* the North's manufactures recorded significant deteriorations ranging from 2.0 to 4.5 per cent per annum. This is a wide range (even wider when allowance is made for confidence limits) but this is in part due to alternative ways of normalising for growth in the total labour force. Even at the lower end of the range the deterioration is emphatic.

Two of these commodities—cotton and sugar—fail by a big margin to satisfy one of the conditions which were said earlier to be needed if the ECDFTT index was to be a good index of incremental inequalisation. The ECDFTT for the other four commodities recorded even more emphatic deterioration, the estimates ranging from 3.5 to 6.0 per cent per annum. In one way it is entirely unsurprising that the four should be much more prone to deterioration since it happens that, with the exception of rubber, they do not face substitutes produced in developed countries, unlike cotton and sugar which do and, as the earlier theoretical reasoning suggested, the presence of substitutes cushions the pressure of other factors towards incremental inequalisation.[5] But in another way it is a little surprising because sugar has not just been subject to heavy protection in the North, it has been subject to automatically adjusting protection such as that afforded by the 'variable levies' of the European Economic Community (tempered by the EEC's commitment to its Lomé convention partners).

For the aggregate of *all* agricultural exportables of the developing countries there is an estimated deterioration of the ECDFTT which ranges from just under 2.0 to 3.25 per cent per annum. As in this case the value of output of agricultural exportables is proxied by the value of agricultural exports and there are no corroborating statistics, the caution that was indicated earlier applies with force. But the result is in keeping with the *a priori* presumption of deterioriation and, in showing a slower deterioration than for the group of four commodities, it is also consistent with the lesser vulnerability expected of exportables which compete against substitutes produced in the North.

The trendlessness of the ECDFTT for minerals (export weight one-quarter) plus the pronounced deterioration of the ECDFTT for agricultural exportables (export weight three-quarters, of which one-half relates to corroborated data) adds up to unmistakable incremental inequalisation for developing countries with respect to the entire pattern of traditional specialisation.

There are of course possible reservations: the wounds can be self-inflicted; the time span of the data is too short; the statistics are fragile; the focusing on exportables can lead to blinkered vision. Most can be dismissed; some deserve to be noted. A discussion of reservations can be found in Chapter VI. Here, apart from reiterating that faster productivity growth in some of the major developing country exportables would have made matters worse, not better, it is worth drawing attention to a benchmark against which the behaviour of the ECDFTT can be compared.

From World Bank data it can be calculated that gross domestic product (GDP) at constant prices per member of the labour force (≡ per head of the economically active population) grew as fast in developing countries during the sixties and seventies as in the developed countries. (If the data were not fragile one could have said perceptibly faster.) This did not avert a slower growth of output per head because for demographic reasons the ratio of dependents to economically active persons moved adversely for developing countries. But conceptually the relative output per member of the labour force is the more appropriate comparator for the ECDFTT. And this comparator suggests that other sectors did not share the inequalising experience of the sectors most closely associated with the traditional pattern of specialisation, a fact which adds weight to the inequalising experience of these sectors.

11. DOUBLE FACTORIAL TERMS OF TRADE (Chapter VII)

If we could net out the employment component of the ECDFTT we would be able to derive a DFTT index which would be very worth having if only because for some policy purposes it is important to know how the observed deterioration of the ECDFTT is shared between productivity and employment. There is, however, an impenetrable data bottleneck with respect to employment in agricultural exportables of developing countries.

12. POLICY (Chapter VIII)

The incremental inequalisation associated with the traditional pattern of trade and specialisation cannot but be viewed with extreme concern by the developing countries. But they would have to grin and bear it if the market forces were doing a good job, for they would not then be able to improve on the market. Indeed, those wedded to the efficiency of markets would say that they could only do worse. But leaving aside any general considerations which in the context of developing countries militate against efficient markets, there is a specific market failure hanging round the neck of traditional exportables characterised by price-inelastic demand, South-dominated production, and largely export-destined output.

In such commodities, as in others, competition impels individual producers to keep availing themselves of opportunities to increase productivity, but under price-inelastic and (in the context of all-round growth) income-inelastic demand the result of their combined endeavour is to decrease price, which through lowering the benefits that they had anticipated, makes the growth of productivity that the market had generated in excess of what is optimal from the collective standpoint of developing countries.[6]

This is saying, in effect, that for an important group of commodities the developing countries are trapped, by the specialisation they inherited, in a situation in which they cannot better their relative position by trying to improve on what they have always done since colonial days and what market forces cause them to be doing in excess anyway.

To repair this flaw in the market mechanism the developing countries need to get together to restrict output. If one country restricted output it would lose while the other producing countries would reap the gain. They must therefore either cartelise unilaterally or participate in an international commodity agreement bilaterally sponsored by exporting and importing countries which contained a price-enhancing element. In the latter case the objective of price enhancement could be limited to stemming, by mutual agreement, the recurring inequalisation effects.

Opposition in the North to such bilateral arrangement is utterly misguided in so far as it rests on the alleged allocative inefficiency of price enhancement, because the theory which concludes that such enhancement imposes a deadweight loss on the world economy also proclaims that the loss will be small relatively to the redistributive effect if demand elasticity is low.

If the North were haunted by the spectre of the South extending unilateral cartelisation beyond petroleum, it would not hesitate to opt for the bilateral solution. It is not so haunted. But in so far as this is so because of the alleged impracticality of cartelisation owing to alternative sources of supply or potential substitutes, this too is misguided, resting on incomplete theory. Only lack of cohesion among developing countries stands in the way of unilateral cartelisation and it is neither diplomatic nor prudent to base policy on the premise that cohesion cannot develop. Recently it has been argued that price enhancement would be pointless, because on Cline's (1980) calculations the world distribution of income at household level would register a barely perceptible improvement by even a quadrupling of price of non-fuel commodities dominated by developing countries. There are two reasons for Cline's unsurprising results: first, in terms of total world income, the transfer from rich to poor countries effected by even a quadrupling of such prices would be minute; second, at household level, distribution within countries swamps any transfers across the developed/developing divide. But the fact that the transfer is small cannot be an argument for making it even smaller or abolishing it. Equally, the fact that internal distribution is important cannot serve as an argument against international redistribution, though it clearly shows that international redistribution is not enough.

Moreover, both reasons are too sweeping. They apply to all transfers, to straight aid as much as to price enhancement. But perhaps this is a good thing. It places the divide between the social values of the antagonists where it should be: the main cleavage is between those who favour more transfers and those who favour less transfers from North to South. The merits of alternative means for increasing the transfers are a legitimate but secondary area of debate.

The emphasis here on price enhancement springs naturally from the subject which this monograph treats and from the need to disperse the theoretical fog which hostility to price enhancement has generated. But if transfer increases by alternative means are found mutually more agreeable by North/South negotiators or if the South can trade off its 'commodity power' for other acceptable methods of transfer, there will be no need to insist on price enhancement.

In any case, price enhancement for traditional exportables is not enough in the long run. Indeed, it is positively insufficient because, in having to be sustained by reduced output and hence reduced employment in those sectors, it adds to the severe unemployment problem of most developing countries. The gain from enhanced prices would outweigh the loss of employment, but nevertheless alternative sources of employment must be sought. This means diversification out of the traditional pattern of specialisation, with manufacturing and home-oriented food production among the most indicated candidates for active promotion.

This is an unsurprising and fitting end. The analysis and evidence point towards incrementally inequalising effects of the traditional North/South trade and specialisation; therefore the ultimate remedy is the dilution of such specialisation.

Note, however, that since incremental inequalisation means inequalisation as compared with some earlier point under the same broad pattern of trade, it cannot serve to rationalise autarky or complete 'delinking' between North and South. (For a review of delinking see Diaz-Alejandro (1978). Moderate delinking is favoured, *inter alia*, by Sid-Ahmed (1981, Chapter X).)

It only remains to add that there is much more work to be done on most of the issues covered in this monograph—a point so obvious that it hardly needs making but which suggests caution, though not timidity, towards its findings.

A memorandum on notation and methodology

A dot over a variable has been used to indicate a percentage change (for example dP/P), whereas the conventional practice is to use a hat ($\hat{P}$), reserving the dot for time rates of growth (as in $\dot{P} = (1/P)dP/dt$). But scaling a variable for time is, in the context of this book, a mere formality which does not affect the qualitative results, so that if $dP/P < 0$, then $(1/P)dP/dt < 0$. It is to emphasise this that the dot convention has been used the way it has.

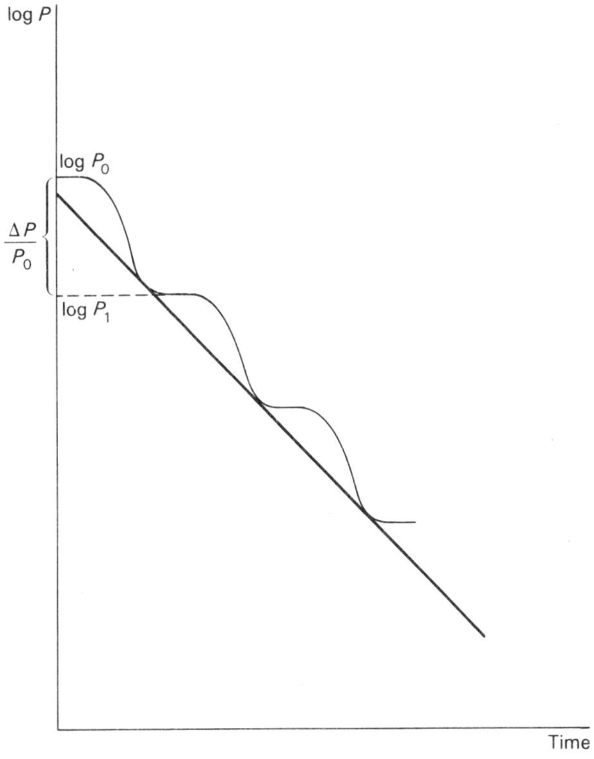

Figure I.1

However, underlying the comparative statics methodology adopted in some parts of this book there is a more general intuitive point: when the system is propelled exogenously, a single exogenous change has comparative statics results which, typically and in relevant respects, will not differ qualitatively from the dynamic results generated by continuous exogenous change. Thus, in Figure I.1, a single exogenous change results in a comparative statics movement from $\log P_0$ to $\log P_1 \equiv \Delta P/P_0 < 0$. Successive repetitions of the exogenous change will generate a path such as is represented by the lightly drawn line. The corresponding path generated by continuous exogenous change is represented by the heavy line—and, clearly, the slope of the heavy line has the same sign as $\Delta P/P_0$ in the comparative statics case.

II

THE THEORY OF DETERIORATING BARTER TERMS OF TRADE SURVEYED

In trying to understand the dissatisfaction of developing countries with the traditional pattern of specialisation, it seems sensible to start with the hypothesis which served to rationalise this dissatisfaction for a couple of decades after World War II and which continues to have many adherents, conscious or subconscious, to the present day: the hypothesis of deteriorating net barter terms of trade (NBTT) for primary products.

The hypothesis was launched by Prebisch (1950) and Singer (1950) and their names have been firmly linked to the hypothesis ever since, particularly the name of Prebisch who repeatedly renewed his commitment to the hypothesis (1951, 1959, 1963, 1964).[1]

The theoretical underpinning which Prebisch and Singer provided over the years is broad based but (unfairly) the part of it which is logically untenable has become especially associated with their names because it is that part which was given prominence when the hypothesis was first launched.

This chapter, which is original only in exposition and interpretation, devotes section 1 to a simple demonstration of the fallacy of this version of the theory. Sections 3-4 turn to the more plausible underpinnings of the deterioration hypothesis and explore their limitations. In section 2 the suggestion is developed that the version which is logically untenable as a long-run theory may hold insights for the short-run behaviour of the relative price of primary products in the context of cost-push inflation originating in industrial countries. Section 5 explores the implications for the NBTT of an elegant Lewis model (1969). Section 6 summarises and concludes.

When Prebisch and Singer launched the deterioration hypothesis after World War II they had to paddle against the main stream of thought. Until then, the dominant *a priori* view regarding the direction of the NBTT between primary products and manufactures was that they would improve. The rationale of this was the diminishing returns stemming from a fixed stock of land (including a fixed stock of mineral deposits of varying accessibility), which would force up primary product prices as population increased and capital was accumulated. Many have asserted the tendency towards improvement of the NBTT of primary products: Ricardo (1821, Chapters II, III and V), Malthus (1820, Chapter III), Torrens (1829, Part 1, Chapter V), J. S. Mill (1896, Book IV, Chapter II), Robertson (1915, p. 169), Keyens (1920, pp. 23-5), Clark (1942, pp. 49-54), Robinson (1954, p. 456); Marx (1844, p. 96) acknowledged it at one time and, among eminent Marxists, Bukharin (1930) was convinced of it, though, unlike the others, he attributed it to 'the monopoly of land ownership' (p. 91).

It is a measure of the achievement of Prebisch and Singer (aided by some long-run statistics assembled in a United Nations (1949) document of which Singer was the principal, though anonymous, author) that they instantly changed the orientation of the debate: those who contested their position did not attempt to argue that there was reason to expect an improvement in the NBTT of primary products, only that no generalisation could be made about such a markedly heterogeneous group of commodities. (See, *inter alia*, Haberler (1959, 1961), Morgan (1959-60), Viner (1953, pp. 111-15).

Prebisch viewed the hypothesis of deterioration as applicable to all primary products regardless of whether they were predominantly produced by developed or developing countries. But for somebody who was so emphatic about the asymmetries between 'Centre' (developed countries) and 'Periphery' (developing countries) this was surely aberrant thinking. His appeal to the universally acknowledged fact that agricultural product prices in the United States had been persistently below their pre-1913 'parity' *vis-à-vis* the price of goods purchased by American farmers (Prebisch 1963) was an irrelevancy. The Prebsich-Singer hypothesis relates to the NBTT of primary products *vis-à-vis* manufactures, whereas the goods purchased by US farmers include services. This makes a big difference because the relative price of services has risen steeply. A more relevant statistic is that the unit value of US agricultural exports had risen relatively to that of US exports of manufactures by some 7 per cent over the period 1913-60 (Lipsey 1963, pp. 451-2; 469-70). No evidence of deterioration here.

For the present purpose the hypothesis of deterioration will be understood to be confined to primary products predominantly exported by developing countries. This is needed, if only because the most plausible of the arguments for deterioration examined in section 3(b) depends on it.

For convenience of exposition the bulk of the discussion will proceed as if all primary commodities were reproducible goods. If a presumption cannot be established that the NBTT will deteriorate for reproducible primary commodities, *a fortiori* it cannot be established for exhaustible natural resources. The price of the latter contains a pure royalty element which must increase at a compound rate equal to the interest on alternative assets, since at the margin the owners have the option of leaving the resource in the ground or extracting it and investing the royalty element of the proceeds.

Effectively cartelised primary commodities, and notably petroleum, are excluded from the argument. Excluding petroleum, the reproducible primary products dominate the primary exports of developing countries. In 1970 the value of their agricultural exports (deemed to be reproducible) was nearly three times that of their (exhaustible) mineral exports other than petroleum.

1. THE FALLACY

As first propounded by Prebisch (1950, p. 6) the theory had essentially one strand, which was also the dominant strand in Singer's (1950) more comprehensive approach: in developed countries increases of labour productivity in manufacturing were reflected in higher incomes; in developing countries increases in labour productivity in primary production were reflected in lower prices (Prebisch 1950, p. 6); as productivity grew continuously, so the NBTT of primary products deteriorated cumulatively.

Prebisch (1950, p. 6) referred to the high degree of organisation of workers in developed countries and their lack of organisation in developing ones as the source of the asymmetry, but he could have blamed it equally on the oligopolistic practices of employers in developed countries. Be that as it may, the essence of it is that competition governs the price of primary products[2] and market-clearing mechanisms force it down when productivity increases, whereas para-market forces—be they labour unions or oligopolistic pricing practices—prevent this from happening in the case of manufactures. This purports to lead directly to the conclusion that the NBTT tend to move against primary products over time.

The conclusion does not, however, follow. The NBTT are a ratio of two money prices. If the money price in the denominator (the price of manufactures) is anchored at a certain level by non-competitive practices, but the money price in the numerator (the price of primary products) is free to be determined by competitive market forces, the denominator can be fixed at any arbitrary level but market forces will cause the numerator to adjust to it at the market-clearing relative price (which may embody a given level of monopolistic market power on the side of manufactures), provided equilibrium exists and is unique.

Prebisch did not confine himself for long to this stark initial version of the theory. Nevertheless it is worth inspecting this version more closely, notwithstanding the numerous criticisms to which it has already been subjected—Haberler (1959, 1961, 1964), Meier (1963, pp. 60-1), Flanders (1964), Johnson (1967, p. 250), Pincus (1967, pp. 131-2), Streeten (1974)—because it keeps popping up all the time. Kaldor (1964) espoused the theory in its stark initial version;[3] textbooks often restrict their account to this version—Meier and Baldwin (1957, p. 234), Baldwin (1966, pp. 54-5);[4] even the editor of the *Essays in Honor of Raul Prebisch*, reviewing Prebisch's contribution from the perspective of the 1970s, relies almost exclusively on this version (Di Marco, 1972) and this is replicated by Cardoso (1977) (writing in a journal edited by Prebisch himself), Palma (1978) and others.[5]

For a closer inspection we need to strip the argument to its essentials and exclude by assumption all factors which may contribute to NBTT deterioration but are irrelevant to this version of the argument. To this end we need to assume: a two-region world, one region producing only a manufactured good (M) and the other only a primary commodity (C); constant employment in each region and labour immobility across regions; exogenous and costless technical progress reflected in the rate of growth of labour productivity (≡ output per employed person); equal rate of productivity growth in both regions/occupations; unity income elasticity of demand for both products; wage proportional to value added per employed person so that the share of wages is constant in regional income; macroeconomic equilibrium, which requires whatever savings ratio would sustain the capital formation implicit in the exogenous technical progress and the postulated productivity growth rate.

Let us kick off by postulating a certain growth of productivity which by assumption must be equal in both C- and M-production. Suppose the relative price or NBTT between C and M ($\equiv P_c/P_m$) is unchanged. Output of both C and M will increase by the same proportion and, therefore, so will world real income. Since income elasticities are all unity, demand for C and M will also increase by the same proportion and the market for both will just clear. The unchanged relative price is sustainable and there is obviously no deterioration of the NBTT.

As there is only one relative price, the general equilibrium outcome can be illustrated with the simplest of Marshallian diagrams. In Figure II.1 the demand and supply schedules for C in the initial situation are labelled D_0 and S_0. The latter is vertical because employment is assumed constant. The growth of productivity displaces the supply schedule to S_1. The demand schedule shifts horizontally by the same percentage to D_1 because world income has increased at the same rate as productivity and income elasticity = 1. The new equilibrium E_1 occurs at the same relative price as the initial equilibrium E_0. Note that this result is independent of the price elasticity of the demand schedule.

Let us examine how the conclusion that there will be no change in the NBTT will be affected if the initial price response to the increase in productivity is asymmetrical along Prebsich-Singer lines. In the manufacturing region money incomes rise in proportion to Π_m^* ($\equiv$ productivity in manufacturing) so that P_m does not change, but P_c falls

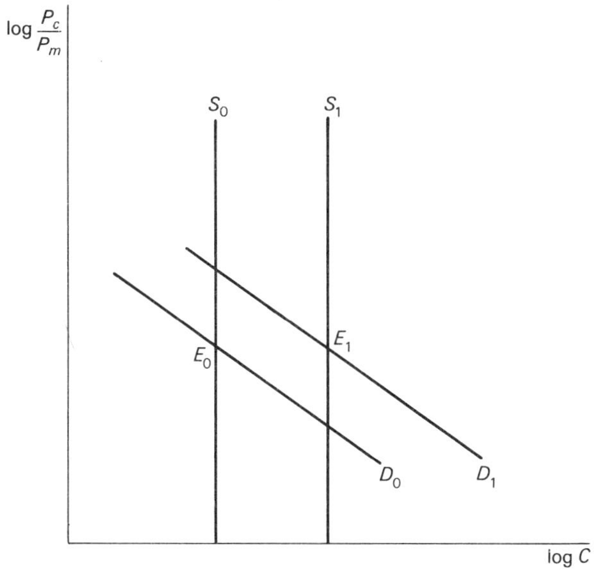

Figure II.1

by the same percentage as the increase in Π_c ($\equiv$ productivity in the commodity sector). The NBTT have deteriorated—but the market will not be cleared; there will be excess supply of *M* and excess demand for *C*. One possible market-clearing mechanism is that output and employment should fall in manufacturing. The deterioration in the NBTT would then persist. But nobody could seriously suggest secularly increasing unemployment in the manufacturing region as the foundation for a theory of secularly deteriorating NBTT. Another market-clearing mechanism is that employment in *C*-production should expand so that the output of *C* grows by more than Π_c. This will be examined later in section 3(b). For the time being it is ruled out by assumption.

The only other plausible market-clearing mechanism is that P_c should rise above the level to which it fell initially. P_m cannot change; it is anchored by the practice whereby productivity increases are taken out in the form of higher incomes. But P_c is determined by supply and demand, it will therefore rise in response to excess demand and it will go on rising until the initial NBTT are restored, because only then will the excess demand disappear. This is the case illustrated in Figure II.1.

The premises cannot therefore sustain the burden of the conclusion Prebisch derived from them. Nothing can be established about a relative price by a hypothesis which anchors down the denominator of a ratio but lets the numerator be market determined.

The initial price ratio was obviously affected by the degree of monopoly or market power at the command of manufacturing firms. The result just derived—that the price ratio would not change under the postulated assumptions—depends on the manufacturing firms' market power being unchanged. If their market power increased the relative price of *M* would rise (of *C* fall), but a continuous deterioration of the NBTT of commodities requires a *continuously* increasing degree of monopoly in manufacturing. The latter may not be inconsistent with the facts, but has not been emphasised by serious proponents of the deterioration hypothesis except in one strand of thought, the consideration of which will be deferred until section 3(c), that has emphasised growing monopolistic power of labour. (Continuously declining market power of commodity producers would have an analogous effect on the NBTT, but it was an essential premise for Prebisch that primary products were competitively priced right from the beginning.)

2. THE THEORY IN THE CONTEXT OF INFLATION

The basic point of the preceding section was that deteriorating NBTT, as envisaged in the initial version of the theory, were not consistent with a market-clearing relative price. Thus the argument was tied to states of equilibrium.

In this section the same version of the theory will be looked at in the context of disequilibrium generated by inflation. The rapid inflation of 1974-5 in developed countries coincided with a sharp deterioration of the relative prices of non-cartelised primary products (from a short-lived peak attained in late 1973 to early 1974), a phenomenon to which a cause-and-effect relation was attributed by developing countries on the basis of Prebisch-type ideas, and which gave great impetus to demands for 'indexation' of primary products.

It has been argued (Spraos, 1977) that in analysing this problem it is essential to distinguish between demand inflation and cost inflation. Suppose that, after a period of equilibrium, all-round excess demand supervenes. P_c will then rise faster than P_m if, as is generally believed, primary product prices are the less sticky of the two. As this will reduce the excess demand for C and increase it for M, the effect will be to erode gradually the inflexibility of prices of manufactures and these will start to catch up. But in the meantime there will be a temporary improvement in the NBTT of commodities. Clearly, this is contrary to the Prebisch prediction.

However, it is cost inflation which is more in keeping with the Prebisch hypothesis. Instead of, as in the previous section, money incomes in manufacturing being pushed up at the same rate as productivity growth, they are pushed up at a higher rate. P_m will now be the first to rise. This will create excess supply of M and excess demand for C; P_c will therefore be pulled up, but in successive rounds of cost inflation (abetted as necessary by an accommodating monetary expansion), P_m may well keep one step ahead, albeit a small step on account of the flexibility of primary product prices. The Prebisch mechanism will then be vindicated: for the duration of the disequilibrium phase some deterioration of the NBTT will persist. But note that it will not be a cumulative deterioration.

If the policy response to cost inflation is to contract real aggregate demand, the deterioration of the NBTT will be reinforced. Indeed this influence, which is somewhat extraneous to the Prebisch mechanism, will be expected to be the more powerful of the two, since primary product prices are more sensitive than those of manufactures to changes of demand.

This story can be told diagrammatically with a view to commenting on an econometric result which bears on this problem. In Figure II.2 points E_t, E_{t+1}, and E_{t+2} represent successive points of equilibrium separated in time by inflationary episodes. They all lie on a straight line with a slope of unity, to indicate constancy of the relative price P_c/P_m. If sandwiched between the equilibrium points we have cost inflation, the path from one equilibrium to the next would be roughly as shown by the dashed lines; if demand inflation, as shown by the dotted lines.

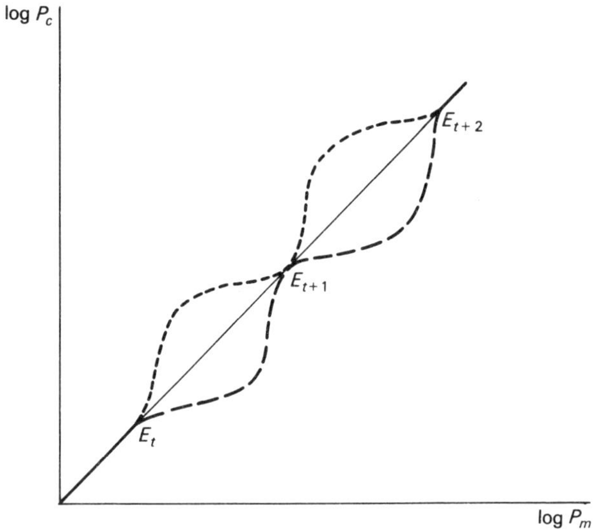

Figure II.2

If now we regress the log of one price on the log of the other, the slope of the regression equation will be close to unity regardless of whether the time path was along the solid line, the dotted line, or the dashed line. If phases on the dotted and dashed lines alternated, the slope would approach unity asymptotically as the inflationary episodes in the sample period increased. In other words, we would be picking up only the long-run relation. The sign of the intercept would reveal whether the dotted or dashed path was dominant, provided that we could identify an equilibrium point, say E_t, and set $P_c = P_m = 100$ at that point. But since typically we cannot do this, no meaning can be attached to the intercept.

Very broadly interpreted, Llewellyn (1974) can be said to have done just such a regression, using quarterly data from 1955 to 1971 inclusive. His conclusion (p. 22) is that: 'The evidence is therefore consistent with the hypothesis that primary prices keep up with any change in the rate of industrial inflation . . .'. If he had added 'in the long run' after 'keep up' his conclusion would still have been consistent with his evidence and more in keeping with the position taken in this section, where some lag in primary product prices, along Prebisch lines, is acknowledged as a plausible disequilibrium phenomenon in a period of cost inflation.

It must now be added that underlying this analysis is the unhistorical approach of much economic theory which treats the long-run equilibrium as independent of the intervening short runs. If we abandon for a brief moment this convenient but questionable approach, we can ask how the disequilibrium associated with cost inflation, which yields for a time a Prebisch-type situation, affects the long run. Presumably it will do so by exerting an influence on the allocation of resources some of which, once channelled to a certain sector, will tend to be anchored there after becoming sector specific. To follow this up we need to allow for some mobility of resources.

If factors of production are attracted by higher relative prices, then, in the course of cost inflation, there will be an expansion of M-production beyond what would have happened in the absence of cost inflation. The long-run effect of this, once cost inflation subsides, will be to lower P_m and hence improve the NBTT of primary products. Thus, a short-run pro-Prebisch result is followed by a long-run anti-Prebisch result. On the other hand, if factors are attracted by excess demand, the position will be reversed: in the cost inflation phase there will be an expansion of the primary sector and in the long run the NBTT of primary products will be less favourable.

Hereafter the analysis reverts exclusively to market-clearing equilibrium situations. But let it be said in passing that whether or not inflation affects the NBTT of primary commodities as a whole, it increases emphatically the relative price variance of individual commodities (see Cline (1981)). The same is true for individual manufactures (see Vining and Elbertowski (1976)) but, while comparisons between primary goods and manufactures have not been made on this score, the increase in the risk borne by individual primary-producing countries is doubtless greater than that borne by industrialised countries, since the product mix of the former is much less diversified.

3. PLAUSIBLE ARGUMENTS

When the assumptions of section 1 are relaxed, a continuing deterioration of the NBTT of primary products may emerge.

(*a*) *Income inelasticity*

Consider the empirically highly plausible case of less than unity income elasticity of demand for *C*. Given the assumption that productivity grows equally in both *M*- and *C*-production, the horizontal shift of the demand function in Figure II.1 will now be smaller than the shift of the supply function and the relative price of primary products will end up lower than before. This will be repeated as productivity continues to grow in successive periods at a rate still assumed to be the same in both occupations.

Singer (1950) introduced income-inelastic demand as a factor contributing to relative price deterioration right from the beginning. Prebisch (1951, p. 50) did the same a year after first launching the deterioration hypothesis, but only implicitly in an arithmetical example which purported to show that supply creates its own demand in manufacturing but not in primary production. Some years later, in the most academic of his writings, Prebisch (1959) gave to income inelasticity the greatest prominence. (In the same paper he dropped completely the fallacious argument described in section 1 and, in so far as he subsequently resurrected it, he did so in less crude forms.)

Income inelasticity of demand for most primary products is very strongly borne out by empirical research. This common feature may be the answer to those of Prebisch's critics who have had much sport at his expense for believing that he could generalise about a collection of commodities which happened to be classified as primary but which were markedly heterogeneous. But while income inelasticity is indeed a common characteristic of primary commodities and does push powerfully towards deterioration of their NBTT, it is not a sufficient condition for deterioration to prevail. This will emerge shortly.

For the moment, revert to unity income elasticity all round but allow for unequal productivity growth. If productivity grows faster in *C*-production, the demand shift in Figure II.1 will be smaller than the supply shift, since demand will shift in proportion to the growth of world income and world income will grow in proportion to the weighted average of productivity growth rates in the two regions. The relative price of C will deteriorate again.

But, of course, the reverse will be the case if C-productivity grows more slowly than M-productivity.

If now C was subject to both income-inelastic demand *and* faster productivity growth than manufactures, there would be downward pressure on the relative price of C from both sources and the deterioration hypothesis would have the fairest possible wind in its sails.

But if income inelasticity was combined with lagging productivity growth in C-making, the result would depend on the relative strength of the two forces. More precisely (as note 6 will establish) the NBTT of C will improve, remain constant or deteriorate according as

$$\frac{\epsilon_c^g}{\epsilon_m^g} \gtreqless \frac{\dot{\Pi}_c}{\dot{\Pi}_m^*},$$

where $\epsilon \equiv$ income elasticity of demand (dimensionally world-wide, hence the superscript g, for global); $\dot{\Pi} \equiv$ percentage growth of productivity; and the subscripts c and m assign, as before, the coefficients to commodities and manufactures respectively, while the star denotes a coefficient appertaining to the manufacturing regions.[6]

This is one of the central results of the vast literature stimulated by Hicks's (1953) 'Inaugural Lecture'—see, *inter alia*, Johnson (1955, 1959), Kemp (1955), Bhagwati (1958), Johnston and Tolley (1965), de Figueroa (1969), Lewis (1972), and Findlay (1981).

Given that empirically $\epsilon_c^g/\epsilon_m^g < 1$ (by virtue of $\epsilon_c^g < 1$, which in a two-good model implies $\epsilon_m^g > 1$), the ratio $\dot{\Pi}_c/\dot{\Pi}_m^*$ is obviously critical. If low enough, it would more than offset the income inelasticity factor and lead to failure of the deterioration hypothesis.

It is an open question of how vexing a qualification this is for a protagonist of the deterioration hypothesis. He could retreat to a conditional version of the hypothesis: the NBTT of the primary-producing region would deteriorate if that region were to grow as fast as the manufacturing region (which under constant employment, implies $\dot{\Pi}_c/\dot{\Pi}_m^* = 1$). Or he could endogenise productivity growth and argue (plausibly) that competition among primary producers prevents $\dot{\Pi}_c$ from falling to very low levels and makes it unlikely that it will lag so far behind $\dot{\Pi}_m^*$ as to offset the pressure towards deterioration of the NBTT which emanates from low income elasticities of demand for primary commodities.

A third way out, more in the spirit (but perhaps not the letter) of Prebisch's position is to recall that he was interested in deteriorating terms of trade as the mechanism whereby 'the peripheral countries transferred . . . a share of the fruits of their own technical progress' (Prebisch, 1950, section II) and to note that failure of the deterioration hypothesis was most likely to occur in circumstances which should be of least interest to him because the productivity gains which were at risk were low anyway.

We can complicate the story by dropping the restriction of regional specialisation. Let both *C* and *M* be produced in both regions and let there be some mobility of labour between *C*-making and *M*-making inside each region. The qualitative results previously established will not be affected. But quantitatively the adverse effect of income inelasticity on the NBTT for primary products is mitigated and the effect of differential productivity growth may be either mitigated or aggravated. These points can be established in the following way.

Assume that the rate of growth of *C*-productivity is equal in both regions and similarly for *M*-productivity. (This need not, of course, imply that the absolute level of productivity is the same in the two regions in either *C* or *M*.) In the first instance let the growth of productivity be the same for *C* and *M* but let demand be income-inelastic for *C* and hence income-elastic for *M*. Productivity growth will generate excess supply of *C* at the initial relative price, which will therefore change adversely for *C*. But the relative price movement will cause income per head in *C*-making to decline relative to that in *M*-making, which will induce some movement of labour from *C* to *M* in both regions. This, in turn, will mitigate the excess supply of *C* and its relative price will not have to fall as much as when labour was completely immobile. So income inelasticity still acts as a force pushing the relative price of *C* towards deterioration, but less so than in the case of complete regional specialisation. However, in the limiting case of perfect labour mobility between *C* and *M*, the relative price will be restored to its initial level and there will be no deterioration.

Now, to focus on differential productivity growth, reverse the assumptions: income elasticity is unity for both goods but productivity grows faster in *M*. The relative price of *C* will now improve. If the percentage improvement is smaller than the difference between the *M*- and *C*-productivity growth percentages, relative income per head in *C*-making will decline and there will be an outflow of labour to *M*-making, which will reduce the supply of *C* and enhance further its price. This is the aggravation case. But if the relative price movement overcompensates for the lower productivity growth in *C*-making, there will be an inflow of labour into the *C* sector and the relative price movement in favour of *C* will be restrained thereby. This is the mitigation case. If mobility is perfect the relative price of *C* will end up rising by a percentage that will compensate exactly for its lower productivity growth rate. This will restore real income per head in the *M* and *C* sectors to their initial relativity, a result which necessarily follows when mobility is perfect.

But, save for the limiting case of perfect labour mobility, income inelasticity and relatively slow productivity growth continue to exert their opposing influences on the NBTT of primary products, as they did in the case of complete regional specialisation.

(*b*) *Pressure of excess labour*

When he returned to the deterioration hypothesis after its initial launch, Prebisch (1951) gave pride of place to the pressure of labour supply on the real wage in developing countries. To simplify the analysis of this point we can revert, without loss, to the assumption that *M* is produced only in one region and *C* only in the other.

In the limiting case of 'unlimited supply of labour', there is infinitely elastic supply of labour of the *C*-producing sector at some given real wage (thanks to the pool of labour in open or disguised unemployment in developing countries) and this leads inexorably to a deterioration of *C*'s relative price.[7]

Let us illustrate this by following the Prebisch–Singer asymmetrical price response described in section 1 but now viewed in the context of unlimited supply of labour. The price of *M* remains constant because the growth of money incomes matches the growth of productivity in *M*-making, but the price of *C* falls in proportion to the growth of *C*-productivity. Initially there is, as before, excess demand for *C* but instead of this pulling up its price, *C*-production draws to itself as much labour as is needed to satisfy the excess demand at a now less favourable NBTT.

Note that this is not dependent on money income per head rising in proportion to productivity in *M*-making. Suppose it rose less, yielding a lower absolute price for *M*. The real wage in *C*-production at which the supply of labour is infinitely elastic would then correspond to a lower money wage (provided *M* enters the *C*-producers' consumption basket) and this would lower the absolute price of *C*, leaving the change in the NBTT the same—which makes it clear that the practice of raising money incomes in *M*-making proportionately to, or more or less than, the growth of *M*-productivity only affects the absolute price level in the long run, not the terms of trade.

Diagrammatically the story is told in Figure II.3. Assuming for expository convenience that *C*-producers consume only *M*, a locus of constant real income per head equal to some arbitrary initial level is given by the line $\overline{YY}$ with slope $= -1$.[8] With initial real income defined by productivity level $\Pi_{c(0)}$ and NBTT $= (P_c/P_m)_0$, the infinitely elastic supply function for commodities will be S_0. (In addition to infinite elasticity of labour supply this requires that cooperant factors of production should not be subject to bottlenecks which give rise to diminishing returns.) When productivity rise to $\Pi_{c(1)}$ the supply function shifts to S_1 and it can be seen at sight that no matter how big the associated shift of the demand function might be, the new equilibrium E_1 will be at a lower relative price for *C* than E_0.

Lewis (1953), who invented the term 'unlimited supply of labour', considered the implications of the concept for the terms of trade and had no difficulty in concluding that it would imply their deterioration for *C* unless other supply bottlenecks intervened. The reason why Lewis's name did not immediately become associated with the deterioration hypothesis is that, except for some tropical agricultural products, he was of the opinion that other bottlenecks did intervene (e.g. limited stock of mineral deposits) diluting the influence of unlimited labour supply on price (Lewis, 1953, p. 184; 1955, p. 281; 1965, p. 484).

Myrdal is sometimes bracketed with Prebisch and Singer as an upholder of the deterioration thesis.[9] In so far as he did have a commitment to this thesis—and it was never strong[10]—it too was founded on the pressure of labour supply.

But how far does the deterioration conclusion carry over if we move away from the limiting case of infinitely elastic labour supply?

Assume now a positive but finite labour supply elasticity with respect to real income per head in *C*-production. This is graphed in Figure II.4 as a positively sloped supply function S_0, drawn through point *A* on the $\overline{YY}$ line (which has the same properties as in Figure II.3) because point *A* lies perpendicularly above the initial productivity level in *C*-making ($\Pi_{c(0)}$). When *C*-productivity rises to $\Pi_{c(1)}$ the supply function must shift in such a fashion as to go through *B* because real income per employee being the same in *B* as in *A*, the supply of labour

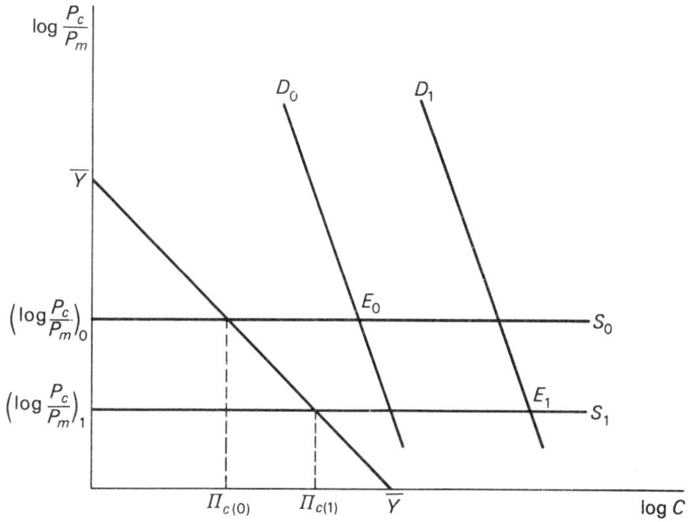

Figure II.3

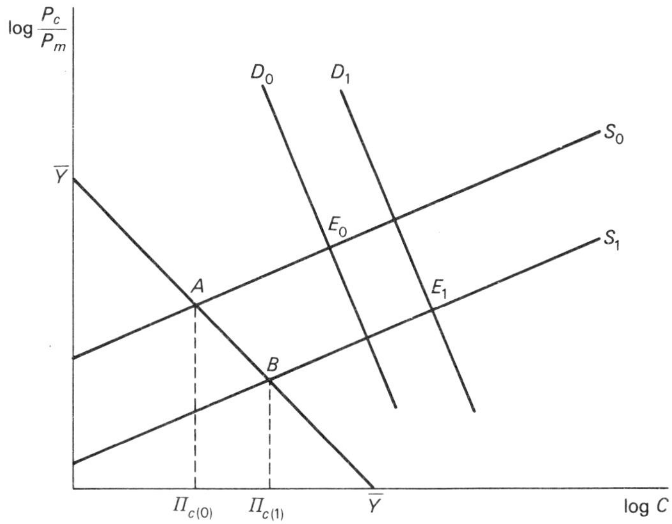

Figure II.4

at that point would be expected to be unchanged and hence output supplied will be higher in proportion to the growth of productivity. If at the same time the demand function shifts from D_0 to D_1 by a horizontal distance equal to productivity growth (i.e. $= \Pi_{c(1)} - \Pi_{c(0)}$), it is geometrically inevitable that at the new equilibrium level E_1 the relative price of C would be lower than at E_0.

Thus the deterioration result carries over to this case. It is an interesting case because it corresponds to what happens when productivity growth in M (and hence world income at unchanged relative price and levels of employment) is the same as in C and income elasticity of demand is unity. Under these assumptions the demand function shifts in the same proportions as productivity growth. In Figure II.1 this led to unchanged terms of trade. It now leads to a deterioration for C because of the pressure exerted on supply by additional labour seeking employment in C-production as real income per head in the C-sector rises.

But clearly the deterioration result is in jeopardy in circumstances which would cause C-demand to shift more than in porportion to C-productivity growth. This could happen if demand for C was income-elastic, which may be ruled out as empirically implausible, or if productivity growth was faster in M than in C.

To get a feel of the weights carried by labour supply elasticity and relative productivity growth rates, respectively, it is convenient to exclude the influence of income elasticity differences by assuming unity elastic demand for both C and M. We then obtain (as shown in note 11) the result that the NBTT of C will improve, remain unchanged or deteriorate according as

$$\frac{\dot{\Pi}^*_m - \dot{\Pi}_c}{\dot{\Pi}_c} \gtreqless e_c,$$

where $e_c \equiv$ elasticity of labour supply with respect to the real wage.[11]

If $e_c = 0$ and $\dot{\Pi}_c = \dot{\Pi}^*_m$, the NBTT will be unchanged: both these assumptions and the result correspond to those of section 1. If $e_c = \infty$, it dominates unequivocally (unless $\dot{\Pi}_c = 0$) and the NBTT of primary products must deteriorate. If $e_c < \infty$, it may be outweighed; but typically e_c would be expected to dominate even when it is quite small. For example, if $\dot{\Pi}^*_m = 5$ per cent and $\dot{\Pi}_c = 2$ per cent, $e_c > 1.5$ is enough for deterioration. The dominance of e_c is, however, jeopardised when $\dot{\Pi}_c$ is very small.

We may conclude that if, as Baer (1969, pp. 206-7) imputes to him but without citing evidence, Prebisch had nailed infinite labour supply elasticity to his mast he would have had a logically watertight case. But even with a labour supply elasticity well to this side of infinity the deterioration result typically carries over, except when $\dot{\Pi}_c$ is very small, in which case there would be little productivity gain of which the periphery could be deprived by a deterioration of its terms of trade.

The criticisms to which Prebisch is open in the present context are different. First, when the deterioration of the NBTT is sustained by an inflow of hitherto unemployed or underemployed labour, the welfare outcome is ambiguous and the NBTT deterioration is not necessarily to be deplored. Second, the pressure of excess labour would affect adversely the NBTT of the periphery regardless of whether its exports were primary products or manufactures. (Singer (1958, 1974), but apparently not Prebisch, was converted to this position.)

(*c*) *A digression on dynamic unequal exchange*

The core of the unequal exchange thesis as developed by Emmanuel (1972 and numerous sequels) relates not to a trend towards deterioration in the terms of trade but to the level at which exchanges between developed and developing regions are taking place at a point of time: exchange is said to be unequal if wages in the two regions are unequal.

Wage differences can, of course, serve as a measure of inequality, But Emmanuel views them as a *source* of inequality. Real wages are the exogenous element on which everything else hinges, including the NBTT which both reflect and validate wage inequality.

In order to make wage inequality the analytical backbone of the unequal exchange thesis it is necessary that equal wages be a feasible option within the given framework. Emmanuel appreciates this and is not put off his stride by it. But nearly everybody else has balked at the idea that, if only it were possible to decree that real wages in the Indias and Bangladeshes of this world be raised by a large enough multiple, a new equilibrium free of unequal exchange in the Emmanuel sense would be established after some transitional frictions.

To get round this implausibility Amin (1976) and others have proposed a modified criterion: unequal exchange is present if wages are more unequal than can be accounted for by productivity differences. But while this attenuates the overimaginativeness of Emmanuel, its logic is irreparably flawed.[12]

The nature of the flaw can, however, be left to a footnote because, by concerning itself with the situation at a point in time, the unequal exchange thesis is not central to this chapter or this book and has been brought into view only to serve as a background to a development which Emmanuel (1979) has christened 'dynamic unequal exchange' and which has implications for the trend of the NBTT that deserve serious consideration. Compare Bell (1979) and Sau (1978, p. 60).

There are two stylised facts in Emmanuel's conception which are critical for the present purpose: (a) continuously growing trade union power in the *M*-producing regions while unions are non-existent or powerless in the *C*-producing regions; (b) immobility of labour between *M*- and *C*-producing regions but perfect capital mobility which equalises rates of profit on capital regardless of location. Any similarity between Prebisch and Emmanuel with respect to (a) is superficial. For Prebisch, the market power of trade unions stands at a given level and this can maintain constant the share of wages in value added but cannot raise it. For Emmanuel, the market power of trade unions is steadily growing and raises labour's share.

Almost any plausible model which incorporates (a) and (b) will yield a presumption of deteriorating NBTT for *C*. (But see Gibson (1980).) If one looks at costs, the relative cost of *M* will rise as real wages in *M*-making rise at a faster rate than exogenous productivity growth. If one looks at excess demand, a relative price which clears the market in one period will be associated with positive excess demand for *M* in the next period, as capital is driven out of *M*-making where returns are being squeezed by real wage push, and equally associated with negative excess demand for *C*, the supply of which is being boosted by migrating capital and boosted all the more if the latter is complemented by previously idle labour.

The growing market power of trade unions which enables them to raise labour's share in the value added in *M*-making is critical. Without it, a money wage push in excess of productivity growth would lead in the long run to pure inflation, with little effect on relative prices.

Nevertheless, in Emmanuel's conception the growth in labour's share in value added in the *M*-making sector is small *ex post*, the reason being that the improvement in the NBTT is the principle source from which at the end of the day faster growth in real wages than in productivity is validated. This improvement makes possible the continuing operation of this process over a long period without capitalism collapsing from a rapidly declining rate of profit.

Whether or not empirically tenable, the logic of the argument is beyond reproach. However, if the capital which migrates into the *C*-making region is complemented by previously unemployed labour, the situation shades into that considered in the preceding subsection and, as there, it may be pointed out that a NBTT deterioration, or from Emmanuel's preferred opitcal angle, an increasing real wage inequalisation, is not an unambiguous relative welfare signpost since it fails to take into account the additional employment which is generated by the very process which inequalises wages.

4. EXTENSIONS

(*a*) *Lewis, vintage 1969*

When a third good is introduced into the model the story becomes more complicated but some basic insights can be gleaned from a special case which has been beautifully articulated by Lewis (1969, pp. 17-22).

Lewis's model bears a close resemblance to that of the preceding pages. There are two regions: developed and developing. The former produces and exports manufactures (M); the latter produces and exports primary commodities (C). The new element is that primary commodities are now defined as exclusive of what constitutes a third good called 'food' (F). Both regions produce F (grains, rice, etc.), which is also traded and therefore its price (P_f) must be the same across regions, there being no transport costs or other barriers to trade.[13] It is immaterial which region exports F and which imports it. Labour mobility between regions is zero but, and this is why the case is said to be 'special', mobility between sectors is perfect. The size of income and price elasticity of demand are irrelevant for the qualitative conclusions derived from this model, because the results are dominated by the infinitely elastic mobility coefficients which perfect intersectoral mobility implies. Unequal productivity growth rates are, however, critical. The other assumptions are the same as those listed in section 1.

There are now three relative prices: P_c/P_m, P_c/P_f, and P_m/P_f of which two are independent: the third is always implied.

By very simple steps the direction of change of P_c/P_m can be derived. Start with the identity

$$\frac{P_c}{P_m} \equiv \left[\frac{P_c\Pi_c}{P_f\Pi_f} \div \frac{P_m\Pi_m^*}{P_f\Pi_f^*}\right]\frac{\Pi_f\Pi_m^*}{\Pi_f^*\Pi_c},$$

where Π_f stands for productivity in F-production in the developing region and Π_f^* in the developed.

Given the model, this identity can be transformed to

$$\frac{P_c}{P_m} = \text{constant} \times \frac{\Pi_f \Pi_m^*}{\Pi_f^* \Pi_c}.$$

The reason for this is the perfect intersectoral labour mobility. Since $P_c \Pi_c$ represents income per head in the developing country's C-producing sector and $P_f \Pi_f$ the same in its F-sector, if the ratio $P_c \Pi_c / P_f \Pi_f$ deviates from its initial level it will generate massive flows of labour until (via changes in goods prices) the initial level will be restored. Thus perfect mobility keeps $P_c \Pi_c / P_f \Pi_f$ constant. By analogous reasoning $P_m \Pi_m^* / P_f \Pi_f^*$ is also kept constant.

It follows that movements of NBTT between C and M depend on changes in the four productivity levels and nothing else. As before, and for the same reasons, the slower the growth of Π_c relatively to Π_m^*, the less likely that the relative price P_c/P_m will decline. But now, additionally, the relative growth of productivity in the respective food-producing sectors is important and it works the other way round: the lagging region finds the P_c/P_m ratio being pulled in a direction unfavourable to it. An intuitive feel for this can be gained in the following way. Suppose Π_c and Π_m^* grow at the same rate and faster than either Π_f^* or Π_f, while Π_f^* grows faster than Π_f. In order to keep $P_c \Pi_c / P_f \Pi_f$ constant, P_c/P_f must keep falling. Analogously P_m/P_f must keep falling but, because it has the smaller productivity growth gap to bridge, it will be falling at a slower rate than P_c/P_f. Therefore P_c/P_m will be declining.

Although at the time Lewis was interested more in the DFTT than in the NBTT and did not commit himself to a view about the latter, his model makes it possible to infer a presumption of relative price deterioration for C.

The F-producing sector in the developed region is, of course, a source of labour supply for M-production when Π_m^* grows faster than Π_f and, in so doing, generates an incipient tendency towards faster earnings growth in M-production. The additional labour enhances the supply of M and exerts a depressing influence on its price relatively to C. But by a similar mechanism C-production in the developing region draws labour from its own F-producing sector. This pulls the price of C towards deterioration relatively to M. Of the two opposing influences, the latter dominates given Lewis's view that productivity in food-growing was rising much more slowly in developing than developed countries. And it dominates overall, because the other counter-influence, Π_c growth much slower than Π_m^* growth, would not have been rated as empirically very plausible by Lewis who often remarked that the rate of productivity growth in some of the principal export-oriented commodities of developing countries was far too rapid for their own good.

Yet the political economy implications of his analysis are strikingly different from Prebisch's even though it shares the conclusion of NBTT deterioration. For Prebisch, the problem is fundamentally associated with the specialisation in primary production inherited by the developing countries from the colonial and semi-colonial era. For Lewis, the developing countries can only blame themselves, since the problem arises because of the slow growth of productivity in the predominantly home-oriented food-producing sector. Spokesmen of developing countries who have pressed the argument fashioned by Prebisch would have no political interest in the argument constructed by Lewis.

If the perfect mobility assumptions are diluted the income elasticities, which have been eclipsed, come into their own again. Having now three goods means that the income elasticities (including a third one for F) enter the argument in a more complicated way but, given as an empirical fact that the income elasticity for C is smaller than for M, the income elasticities tend in general to push the NBTT of C *vis-à-vis* M in a declining direction.

(*b*) *Other*

Any number of further extensions are possible. The standard neo-classical model with two goods, two fully employed factors and two countries, and with convexity conditions satisfied, can trace through the terms of trade effects of technical progress which can be factor-biased as well as product-biased. It can also trace the effects of exogenous changes in factor endowments and can allow for endogenous variability of factor supplies. It can show that the results are sensitive to this or that violation of Pareto optimality conditions and to this or that factor intensity ranking of the products.

The literature in this vein is vast and the combinations of assumptions and outcomes can be counted in hundreds; nearly two decades ago Pryor (1966) had already identified 162. Yet the present survey can properly come to an end at this point. For these are taxonomic exercises of the 'if this, then that' variety without any implication about which 'this' or what 'that' might be expected to dominate. While they are rendering us a service in emphasising the complexities at the level of minutiae, they do not significantly add to or subtract from the stock of ideas which are associated with the hypothesis of deteriorating NBTT for the primary products of developing countries and which this chapter set out to review.

5. SUMMARY AND CONCLUSIONS

Prebisch and Singer started the hypothesis of deteriorating NBTT for primary products on the wrong foot. The argument that productivity growth is distributed in the form of higher money incomes in manufacturing (developed countries) but in the form of lower prices in primary production (developing countries) is neither necessary nor sufficient to establish the hypothesis. Worse, it does not contribute anything, it is just surplus baggage.

This, however, relates to the long run, for which the hypothesis was intended in the first place. In the shorter run, in phases of disequilibrium associated with episodes of cost-push inflation in developed countries, the Prebisch argument can be defended as a logically valid foundation for a hypothesis of (temporary) deterioration.

However, and notwithstanding the last point, it is unfortunate and a mistake that in much of the literature Prebisch should have been packaged and labelled for eternity with this particular argument. For soon after the initial launching of the hypothesis, he began to underpin it with other more solid and empirically plausible arguments and thereafter rarely committed himself to his initial theory in its starkest and logically most untenable version.

The essential arguments were now two: first, primary commodities suffer from a downward demand bias, the measure of which is their lower income elasticity compared with manufactures; second, they suffer from an upward supply bias because they draw on the pool of excess labour in the less progressive sectors of the developing countries' economies.

A third argument, associated with Emmanuel, is that primary commodities of developing countries have had to contend with the continuously increasing market power of labour unions in developed countries.

These are logically solid arguments and at least the first two have strong empirical underpinning. Yet they are not conclusive and considerations which could push the NBTT in an anti-Prebisch direction must not be overlooked. Three are especially noteworthy.

The first relates to exhaustible resources. They have a built-in price-enhancing element both because they grow more scarce and because, of the known reserves, the most accessible ones are the first to be exhausted. The classical view of the 'niggardliness' of nature has turned out to be too pessimistic regarding agriculture because the land frontier has kept receding thanks to technical progress, but it comes into its own, at least to some extent, in natural resources.

The second arises when technical progress and the consequential growth of productivity is slower in the non-manufacturing sector of developed countries than the manufacturing one. This causes an incipient tendency for earnings in non-manufacturing to lag, which encourages labour to switch to manufactures thereby expanding their supply and depressing their relative price.

The third relates again to differential productivity growth but as between primary production in developing countries and manufacturing in developed countries. If the former lags behind, it has a relative supply-restricting effect on primary products and hence a price-enhancing consequence.

Cartelisation and policy-induced acceleration of industrialisation in primary-producing countries also have price-enhancing consequences for primary products but, as Prebisch has emphasised in one of his later writings (Prebisch, 1976, p. 66), these do not damage his deterioration thesis, which was explicitly developed in the context of competitive markets for developing country products.

The other three considerations would, of course, damage Prebisch if they completely offset forces favourable to his thesis—which in the light of the long-run statistical evidence reviewed in the next chapter they could be interpreted as having done. But the damage is perhaps less than overwhelming. For the counterpart to the first anti-Prebisch consideration is that natural resource-exporting countries are suffering a depletion of their stock of assets for which some compensation in the form of improving terms of trade is needed merely to sustain the initial level of welfare.

As for the second anti-Prebisch consideration, it is the logical counterpart of the pro-Prebisch influence emanating from excess labour in developing countries and cannot be expected, by itself, to overshadow it.

Finally, with respect to the third anti-Prebisch consideration, it needs to be remembered that Prebisch was not interested in the deterioration of the terms of trade *per se* but in the way that they caused the primary-exporting developing countries to be deprived of their productivity gains. If the productivity gains were low anyway, as would be required to sustain an anti-Prebisch terms of trade result, there would not be much to be deprived of and the case would not presumably excite Prebisch.

This last having been said, however, it is something of a mystery why, since Prebisch was interested in the combination of terms of trade *and* productivity changes, he did not attack the problem via the terms of trade concept which embodies this precise combination —the concept of double factorial terms of trade.

III

THE STATISTICAL DEBATE ON THE TREND OF BARTER TERMS OF TRADE

The theory surveyed in the previous chapter, while adducing some powerful arguments in support of the hypothesis of deterioration of the net barter terms of trade (NBTT) of primary products *vis-à-vis* manufactures, is in the last analysis inconclusive because, unsurprisingly, the counter-arguments are not so insubstantial that they can be deemed to be unambiguously dominated.

For further light we turn in this chapter to the statistical evidence and review the intense debate which has revolved round this evidence. The debate has been bedevilled by the inadequacy of the long-run statistics available.

Whereas the hypothesis of a deteriorating trend for primary products enunciated by Prebisch (1950) and Singer (1950) related to the ratio of prices between classes of commodities traded world-wide, the paucity of available statistics for the pre-World War II years pushed Prebisch into relying on the terms of trade evidence of an individual country; and whereas the Prebisch-Singer hypothesis related clearly, if only implicitly, to the primary products in which developing countries had a major interest,[1] the price or unit value data did not distinguish between traded primary products according as they originated from developed or developing countries.

Prebisch (1950), when launching the hypothesis, rested his statistical case on the NBTT of the United Kingdom for the whole of its merchandise trade. He spliced two partially overlapping series[2] to give a run of index numbers from 1876-80 to 1946-7 which showed an unmistakable secular improvement in Britain's terms of trade (see Table III.1, column (1)). Since for a great part of this period Great Britain was the most important exporter of manufactures and importer of primary products, he took this to imply a secular deterioration in the NBTT of primary products as traded world-wide.

The critics came down with great severity on the inappropriateness of the data. Many of their points were already acknowledged at some length in the United Nations paper (UN 1949, appendix A) which Prebisch had indicated as the source of his British data,[3] but they were not less worthy of consideration for not being entirely original.

The principal criticisms were four:

(a) The UK NBTT was not representative of the industrial countries as a whole and hence its inverse could not serve as a proxy for the terms of trade of primary products. (Kindleberger (1956, pp. 261-3; 1958), Meier and Baldwin (1957, p. 234), Haberler (1959, p. 20; 1961), Morgan (1959-60), Meier (1963, p. 59), Lipsey (1963, p. 17), Johnson (1967, p. 249), Bairoch (1975, pp. 114-15), Anell and Nygren (1980, pp. 133-4).)

(b) Primary products imported by industrialised countries included commodities predominantly produced in developed countries. (Meier and Baldwin (1957, p. 235), Meier (1958; 1963, p. 59). Van Meerhaeghe (1969, p. 576), Frank (1976).)

(c) Exports are valued f.o.b. whereas imports are valued c.i.f. (or, where the primary products index is based on prices quoted in commodity exchanges, the prices are frequently for delivery in London, Liverpool, etc.), so the improvement in the UK NBTT could be due partly or even wholly to a reduction in transport costs and not to a relative fall in the prices received by primary producers. (Viner (1953, p. 114), Baldwin (1955), Ellsworth (1956), Meier and Baldwin (1957, p. 236), Meier (1958; 1963, p. 60), Haberler (1959, p. 20; 1961), Morgan (1959-60, 1963), Hyde (1963), Kenwood and Lougheed (1971), Streeten (1974), Bairoch (1975, pp. 115-19), Commonwealth Secretariat (1975, pp. 65-6), Schloss (1977), Macbean and Balasubramanyam (1978, p. 162), Anell and Nygren (1980, pp. 133-4).)

(d) New manufactured goods enter trade and the quality of existing ones is improved, but these developments are not reflected adequately in the price index of manufactures, which therefore tends to be biased upwards and thus gives the impression of a deterioration in the NBTT of primary products where none may be there. (Viner (1953, p. 114), Baldwin (1955; 1966, pp. 55-6). Ellsworth (1956), Meier and Baldwin (1957, p. 236), Meier (1958; 1963, p. 59), Haberler (1959, p. 21; 1961), Morgan (1959-60; 1963), Enke (1963, pp. 464-5), Streeten (1974), Commonwealth Secretariat (1975, pp. 68-9), Schloss (1977), Macbean and Balasubramanyam (1978, p. 162).)

All these are plausible points *a priori*, but are they empirically significant, do they in practice amount to a refutation of the statistical inference of deterioration? This is an obvious question which should have been posed more searchingly than it has been and which will be posed here. The short answer is that a deteriorating trend is detectable in the data for the period 1870-1938—the period over which the heated statistical debate was joined—but is questionable when the period is extended to include the post-World War II decades.

A large part of this chapter will be devoted to the 1870-1938 time span. Although a truncated period like that is of limited practical interest, it would be of great interest to scholars if the record could be straightened and the confusions of a partisan debate ironed out.

Of course, index numbers which go back over so many years suffer from serious conceptual problems and errors of measurement. These will be largely ignored. For the most part it will be taken as a working presumption that the statistical series, all from reputable sources, measure accurately what they purport to measure. In no case, however, do statistical series extending far into pre-World War II years purport to measure directly the NBTT between the totality of primary products predominantly originating in developing countries and the manufactures imported by developing countries from developed countries. The question therefore is whether available series are themselves plausible proxies for the NBTT in question or can throw light on the plausibility of conclusions derived from such proxies.

A methodological point before embarking on the substance of the paper.

Trends will be estimated by semi-loglinear regression of the form

$$\ln(\text{NBTT}) = \text{constant} + rt,$$

where $t \equiv$ time. If we viewed this equation as the super-reduced form of a model (such as that of Chapter V) in which time captures the net effects of complex interactions, it would be meaningful to apply the usual econometric tests to the trend coefficient r. And, indeed, in what follows we would want to check whether the observed trend is significantly different from zero. But really the object is not to 'explain' the observed movement of the NBTT (which would have required *inter alia*, high R^2s), nor to obtain 'efficient' predictors (which would have been vitiated by the presence of autocorrelation), nor even to seek the best fit on time (which would have been obtained by regressing on a polynomial in t). We merely want to elicit whether a trend is present, and in what direction, by estimating r, which gives the 'average' rate of change of the regressand per unit time. From the point of view of the statistical significance of r it is unfortunate but unavoidable that the residuals are autocorrelated. (The Durbin-Watson statistic (not reported individually) is lower than one in every regression on t.) However, in most cases the T-ratios are so high that they could take in their stride an allowance for the exaggerated impression of statistical significance that they convey in the presence of autocorrelation.

1. WAS THE UNITED KINDOM EVIDENCE MISLEADING?

Even before Prebisch launched his hypothesis it was fairly clear that it could not be taken for granted that Britain's experience with its merchandise NBTT was shared by every industrialised country, a paper by Martin and Thackeray (1948) having conveniently assembled some of the available evidence. This was reinforced by Kindleberger (1956), who computed the combined NBTT of the industrialised countries of Europe starting in the 1870s: by roughly netting out the UK, it could be seen that the remaining countries, unlike the UK, experienced no significant trend in their NBTT up to World War II. The subsequent work of Lipsey (1963) on the NBTT of the United States showed (pp. 442-3) that for merchandise trade as a whole the US shared the favourable experience of the UK, but since in the seventy years down to World War II the structure of the trade of the US had changed radically—initial domination of its exports by agricultural products having been replaced by a preponderance of manufactures in the inter-war years—this was of no great help. On the contrary, when the focus is narrowed to the US NBTT between imported primary products and exported manufactures, the resulting series is best described as trendless (Lipsey 1963, pp. 451-2) and the same is true for industrial Europe (Kindleberger 1956, p. 259; 1958).

Furthermore, some long time series with more or less direct bearing on the primary products/manufactures dichotomy which were assembled by Morgan (1959-60) for a mixed bag of seven countries behaved so differently that he concluded that no generalisation could be made and, *ipso facto*, that any generalisation based on British data was illegitimate.

In retrospect it seems odd that Prebisch chose to rest his case on exclusively British data when the UN source from which he obtained them (UN 1949, Table 5) also included a terms of trade series labelled 'Primary to Manufactured Commodities in World Trade'. It is true that this series (first published in graph form in League of Nations (1945) p. 18) was also based on British data up to 1929, but with the important difference that the price index for manufactures was based on both British exports and British imports of manufactures, the latter intended as a proxy for manufactures of non-British origin; and with the further difference that for 1929 and later years the net was cast more widely by using world trade data compiled by the League.

The League series is set out in Table III.1, column (2). The first question is whether Prebisch (1950) seriously misled himself and others by not using the best evidence available at the time. Comparing column (1) of Table III.1 (which was used by Prebisch) with column (2), it can be seen that the trend against primary products is marked in both, though less so in column (2). This is confirmed by the semi-log regressions of the respective series on t reported in rows 1 and 2 of Table III.2. The Prebisch series suggests an annual rate of change of the relative price of primary products of −0.9 per cent; the League series of −0.6 per cent.[4] So, by his choice of series, Prebisch exaggerated the adverse trend for primary products, but the adverse trend was none the less unmistakably present in the League's more appropriate series.[5]

But, of course, the credentials of the League series as a proxy for the primary products/manufactures price ratio in world trade is at this stage open to question. Lewis (1952) tried to improve on the League (1945) by adding to the data pool the prices of imports and exports of manufactures of the US and in other ways. (For details see the second and third notes to Table III.1.) It turns out that his series is highly correlated with the League series (see row 18 of Table III.2). In one sense this is not surprising since the two series were not derived from entirely independent sources. But in another sense it shows the robustness of the League's series, its ability to withstand substantial tinkering without its main message being affected.

Material from heterogeneous sources has been sown up together to construct the statistical series considered hitherto. But more system and greater conceptual homogeneity underlies a long-run series put together by the UN Secretariat (UN, *Statistical Yearbook 1969*, updated in UNCTAD, *Handbook 1972*). It is set out in column (4) of Table III.1. The NBTT in this series measure the unit value of world-wide exports of SITC classes 0–4 and 9 divided by the unit value of world-wide exports of SITC classes 5–8. It is still an imperfect index. The SITC dichotomy adopted approaches—but not very accurately—the primary products/manufactures distinction (most disconcertingly, non-ferrous metals are in class 6); the coverage is only 60–65 per cent

TABLE III.1

Approximations to net barter terms of trade between primary products and manufactures up to 1938

(Price or unit value of primary products ÷ price or unit value of manufactures: 1913 = 100.)

Year	Prebisch* (1)	League† (2)	Lewis‡ (3)	UN § (4)	Year	Prebisch (1)	League (2)	Lewis (3)	UN (4)
1871			103.0		1901			96.1	85
1872			105.2		1902			96.1	88
1873			106.7		1903	101	96	96.0	90
1874			105.5		1904			94.1	90
1875			103.2		1905			92.9	93
1876			103.2		1906			97.1	90
1877			105.9		1907			98.3	88
1878	119	107	102.8		1908	102	97	93.5	93
1879			99.8		1909			95.0	96
1880			100.0		1910			96.0	100
1881			101.6		1911			98.2	103
1882			103.6		1912	101	100	100.3	100
1883	122	106	100.5		1913			100.0	100
1884			97.8						
1885			96.0						
1886			92.6		1921	71	69	70.5	65
1887			94.5		1922	76	75	75.9	76
1888	115	100	95.9		1923	78	83	90.6	87
1889			97.6		1924	82	88	92.4	88
1890			95.6		1925	84	90	93.7	98
1891			95.5		1926	82	88	91.2	91
1892			93.4		1927	82	91	93.0	93
1893	107	97	95.5		1928	84	88	89.2	93
1894			92.8		1929	84	86	88.9	91
1895			89.2		1930	76	77	78.6	72
1896			90.1		1931	69	68	70.5	64
1897			92.3		1932	69	65	65.1	60
1898	104	99	93.5		1933	67	65	66.5	61

1899	}	}	94.8		1934	69	70	72.1	68
1900			98.0	80	1935	70	72	73.2	70
					1936	72	74	77.1	76
					1937	76	79	81.4	82
					1938	70	73	74.7	68

Sources

Column (1): UN, Economic and Social Council, *Post War Price Relations In Trade Between Under-Developed and Industrialised Countries* (New York, 1949 (mimeo), later published as *Relative Price of Exports and Imports of Underdeveloped Countries*, Lake Success, New York, 1949).

Column (2): As for column (1). Based on League of Nations, *Industrialisation and Foreign Trade* (Geneva, 1945).

Column (3): W. A. Lewis, 'World production, prices and trade, 1870–1960', *Manchester School of Economic and Social Studies* (1952, Vol. 20, pp. 105–38).

Column (4): UN, *Statistical Yearbook 1969.*

Notes to Table III.1

* Primary products are proxied by the UK's total merchandise imports and manufactures by the UK's total merchandise exports. Following Prebisch, *The Economic Development of Latin America and its Problems* (UN, New York, 1950), the series is derived by splicing two separate indices given in the source: down to 1913 an index based on Schlote, *British Overseas Trade from 1700 to 1930s* (Oxford, 1952) and thereafter the index of the UK Board of Trade.

† Up to 1929: the Sauerbeck wholesale price index serves as proxy for the price of traded primary products, and a weighted average of British export and import prices of manufactures (derived from Schlote's respective series) as a proxy for manufactures traded world-wide, British exports being given the larger weight. In the 1930s: more global estimates from League of Nations. *Review of World Trade 1938.*

‡ Up to 1913: for primary products, a weighted average of Schlote's index for UK imports of food and a combined index for UK imports and exports of raw materials, the weights being the respective shares in world trade; for manufactures, an unweighted average of Schlote's British exports and imports of manufactures. In the 1920s: for primary products, the unweighted average of UK and US imports of food and raw materials respectively combined into a single index for primary products by weighting according to the shares in world trade of the two sub-categories; for manufactures, the unweighted average of UK and US exports and imports of manufactures. In the 1930s: as for column (2).

§ Built from national indices (estimated by UN staff where not otherwise available) which were weighted according to national shares in world trade. Reweighting was undertaken at intervals and the subperiods were linked through overlapping years. Inside each subperiod initial year weights were used except for post-World War II subperiods (the index numbers for which are given in Table III.3, column (1)) where terminal year weights were used in some cases. Two indices were built, one for total exports and one for manufactures (SITC 5–8). The index for 'primary products' (SITC classes 0–4 and 9) was derived as a residual. Up to 1913 the coverage extended over only 60–65 per cent of world exports (50–55 per cent of exports of primary products).

TABLE III.2

Regression coefficients

Regressand	Regressor: t	D	D'	$NBTT_L$	$NBTT_{UN}$	R^2
1 $NBTT_P$	–0.0095					0.91
1876–1938	(–18.2)					
2 $NBTT_{LN}$	–0.0064					0.74
1876–1938	(–9.6)					
3 $NBTT_L$	–0.0046					0.62
1871–1938	(–9.7)					
4 $NBTT_L$	–0.0028					0.43
1871–1929	(–6.1)					
5 $NBTT_L$	–0.0055					0.82
1871–1899	(–10.9)					
6 $NBTT_{UN}$	–0.0073					0.33
1900–1938	(–3.9)					
7 $NBTT_{UN}$	–0.0005					0.004
1900–1929	(–0.2)					
8 $NBTT_{UN}$	0.0013					0.04
1900–1970	(1.4)					
9 $NBTT_{UN}$	–0.0152					0.95
1950–1970	(–19.3)					
10 $NBTT_{WB(P)}$	–0.0230					0.88
1950–1970	(–11.6)					
11 $NBTT_{WB}$	–0.0110					0.44
1950–1975	(–4.4)					
12 $NBTT_{TAD}$	–0.0157					0.59
1950–1975	(–5.8)					
13 $NBTT_H$	–0.0014					0.04
1900–1970	(–1.5)					
14 $NBTT_L$	–0.0046	0.53				0.89
1871–1938	(–18.0)	(12.1)				
15 $NBTT_L$	–0.0029		0.53			0.89
1871–1938	(–9.6)		(12.0)			
16 AX_{US}	0.0047					0.01
1879–1938*	(0.84)					
17 AM_{US}	–0.0055					0.16
1879–1938*	(–3.2)					
18 $NBTT_{LN}$				1.18		0.95
1876–1938				(22.4)		
19 $NBTT_{LN}$					0.87	0.90
1901–1938					(13.4)	

Symbols

NBTT ≡ net barter terms of trade, distinguished by subscripts as follows: *P* ≡ Prebisch (Table III.1, column (1)); *LN* ≡ League of Nations (Table III.1, column (2)); *L* ≡ Lewis (Table III.1 column (3)); *UN* ≡ United Nations (Table III.1,

[*See opposite page for* Symbols *cont. and* Notes]

of world exports up to 1913 (50–55 per cent for exports of food and raw materials); it does not go back further than 1900. But its conceptual homogeneity is a considerable virtue and it can serve as a test for the League series for the overlapping years.

The UN series is rather more erratic (its exponential trend of –0.7 per cent per annum has a comparatively low *T*-ratio of –3.86; see row 6 of Table III.2) but the League series is still highly correlated with it (row 19, Table III.2). This disguises what appears to be a poor correlation of the two series prior to World War I, but the general picture conveyed by the League series is broadly confirmed by the UN series.

A Chow test confirms that the trend values obtained from the UN and League series respectively do not differ significantly at the 5 per cent level. It may be added that the global data assembled by Maizels (1963), though only for a few key years, corroborate the UN series closely.[6]

The conclusion at this stage must be that the leap from the evidence of Britain's NBTT to an inference about the relative price of primary products *vis-à-vis* manufactures in world-wide trade was not misleading as to direction though it gave an exaggerated impression of the magnitude of deterioration. Britain, by its importance in world trade over the relevant period and the untypically large improvement of its NBTT, had evidently left its mark on the global picture.

---

column (4) and Table III.3, columns (1*a*) and (1*b*)); *WB(P)* ≡ World Bank, including petroleum (Table III.3, column (2)); *WB* ≡ World Bank, excluding petroleum (Table III.3, column (3)); *TAD* ≡ UNCTAD (Table III.3, column (6)); *H* ≡ Hybrid series combining $NBTT_{UN}$ (1900–38) and $NBTT_{WB}$ (1950–70) with 1956 as link year.

AX_{US} and AM_{US} ≡ unit value indices of US agricultural exports and imports respectively. (*Source*: R. E. Lipsey, *Price and Quality Trends in the Foreign Trade of the United States*, Princeton, 1963.)

t ≡ time.

D ≡ logarithmic residual from trend line of world manufacturing output (obtained by fitting a semi-loglinear trend to a series constructed by Lewis for the period 1971–1938—same source as Table III.1, column (3)).

D′ ≡ same as for *D* except that the trend of world manufacturing output was derived by using Lewis's data from 1871 to 1929 only.

Notes to Table III.2

General: all variables are in logs except *t*; constants are omitted: the brackets contain *T*-ratios which are adjusted for grouped data where appropriate.

* The extreme values of the years 1917–20 were omitted from the calculations.

2. WHAT BIAS FROM NOT DISTINGUISHING BETWEEN PRIMARY EXPORTS OF DEVELOPED AND DEVELOPING COUNTRIES?

The point to which attention is now turned was put succinctly by a prominent textbook writer and anthologist when he wrote: 'Nor are the terms of trade between primary products and manufactured products the same as the terms of trade between poor and rich countries' (Meier 1958, p. 286).

As a statement of fact this is right. By not excluding from the calculation primary exports predominantly originating in developed countries, the statistics blur the issue. But as a substantive criticism it is of doubtful validity because the evidence does not point to a lesser deterioration of the NBTT for the narrower range of primary products which originate predominantly in developing countries.

The evidence is indirect. Take first the price data for US agricultural imports and exports. It seems reasonable to assume that the weight of tropical or sub-tropical products was larger in US imports than in exports and hence that the import composition was closer to that of the basket of agricultural exports of developing countries. It follows that if we observed a tendency for the unit value of US agricultural imports to fall more than the corresponding index for agricultural exports, the evidence would strengthen the statistical inference of deterioration. And we do observe this: as shown in rows 16 and 17 of Table III.2, trend-fitting to the series assembled by Lipsey (1963, pp. 151–2) yields a positive (though insignificant) rate of change for the unit value of US agricultural exports and a negative one for imports (both measured f.o.b.).

Other evidence is more neutral. Kindleberger (1956, p. 265) has constructed a unit value index for selected years for industrial Europe's combined exports and imports of primary products (but excluding intra-trade of industrial Europe) which falls by a cumulative 22 per cent from 1872 to 1938. Over the same period his unit value index for industrial Europe's imports of primary products from his 'other' group of countries (essentially Africa except South Africa, Asia except Soviet Asia and Asiatic Turkey, and Latin America except Argentina and Uruguay) falls by 38 per cent. This suggests that the subset of primary products of developing country origin has experienced a bigger price fall, though the difference may not be significant given the sensitivity of such calculations to the choice of initial and terminal years.

Almost perfectly neutral is the evidence of Maizels (1963, p. 88). His unit value index for primary exports of industrial countries as a group (defined in note 6) shows a cumulative rise of 41 per cent from 1899 to 1937, while his unit value index for total exports (dominated, however, by primary products) of all other countries rises by 43 per cent.

Perhaps there exists other evidence which points the other way, but for the time being the conclusion must be that had terms of trade data specific to those primary products in which developing countries have a major interest been available, they would not have weakened the statistical foundation of the deterioration hypothesis.

3. THE PROBLEM OF INCONSISTENT VALUATION

In principle, if freight and insurance costs are a large proportion of the c.i.f. price of primary product imports at the start of a period for which we have observations and they fall heavily during the period, it is possible to observe a deterioration in the NBTT of primary products when these are measured c.i.f. *vis-à-vis* manufactured exports measured f.o.b., whereas the situation which would have been revealed had both been measured f.o.b. was in fact the reverse.

Ellsworth (1956) made a serious attempt to document the presence of a valuation bias and used it as an argument for questioning the meaning of the available NBTT series. His evidence related to the big decline in freight costs which was such a notable event in the economic history of the tail-end of the nineteenth century, thanks to the advent of the steamship. He argued that the whole of the apparent deterioration of the NBTT of primary products in the period 1871-1905 could be accounted for by this factor.

This is a plausible interpretation of the evidence. But a caveat would have been in order—that a bias applicable to the first thirty years of a much longer statistical series might have cancelled out in the remaining years.

For this is what appears to have happened if the series for tramp shipping freights meticulously constructed by Isserlis (1938) is to be believed. In terms of presentation his series has the great merit that he compares it with the Sauerbeck price index, precisely the index used up to 1929 for the primary product prices which went into the calculation of the NBTT series of the League set out in Table III.1, column (2). Figure III.1 replicates one given by Isserlis. There would be no

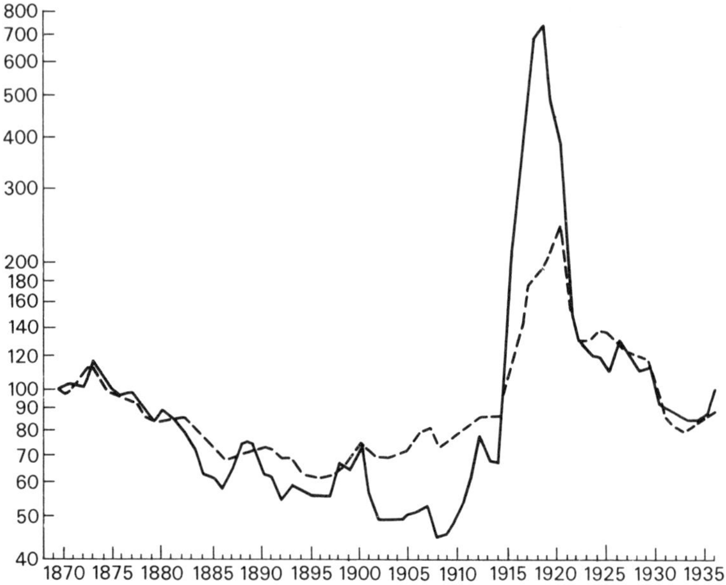

Tramp shipping freights ——
and wholesale prices (Sauerbeck index) — — —, 1869–1936
1869 = 100

Figure III.1

valuation bias, in the sense that an f.o.b. and a c.i.f. index would behave identically, if the Sauerbeck price index and the Isserlis freight index traced the same path on the graph, because this would imply that the freight element would be changing in the same proportion as the f.o.b. price. It can be seen that for the last three decades of the nineteenth century the two indices follow roughly the same path. Then the freight index drops substantially below the price index (which is consistent with Ellsworth's interpretation). But not for long: after an interlude during World War I when the freight index rose violently, the two indices resume their pre-1900 relation. It follows that, according to this series, the charge of a valuation bias for the relevant period as a whole is refuted; a bias in the middle of the period is cancelled in later years.

Kindleberger's freight index (1956, p. 19) behaves in a similar fashion: in the early years it falls drastically relatively to the unit value of industrial Europe's primary imports from the 'other' group of countries; after the first decade of the twentieth century it rises relatively but, unlike the Isserlis index which makes up the whole of the ground lost earlier, Kindleberger's only makes up about half. In Kindleberger's own estimation his index is not satisfactory (1956, p. 336), but if we were to prefer it to Isserlis's index we would be left with some residual validity for the valuation bias, but a small residual when the seventy years down to World War II are taken as a whole.

Bairoch (1975, p. 117) has made an alternative attempt at establishing statistically the presence of a valuation bias by reference to the decline in the difference between the value of world imports of primary products measured c.i.f. and the value of world exports of the same products measured f.o.b. He quotes the difference as being 23.1 per cent in 1876-80 and 10 per cent in 1926-9.

But the belief that the observed difference between values c.i.f. port of destination reported by one country and values f.o.b. port of origin reported by another can be identified with freight and insurance costs is open to question. There are a whole host of other reasons for this difference, all of which may also cause the difference to decline. One illustration of the other sources of difference is provided by the attempt of the statistical services of the US (Department of Commerce) and Canada (Bureau of the Census) to reconcile their respective statistics of the trade flows between the two countries in 1970. Unlike most countries, the US and Canada report their imports as well as their exports f.o.b., so that lack of comparability does not arise on this score, yet non-negligible discrepancies remain. One source of discrepancy identified was the undercounting of exports because they are subject to less control than imports, a factor which was estimated to account for 6 per cent of the f.o.b. value of goods moving from the US to Canada and 1 per cent of the f.o.b. value of the reverse flows.

But quite apart from the statistics, it is relevant to the debate to note that if the unit cost saving from progress in transportation technology was equal to the relative fall in the c.i.f. price of primary products, it would mean that the importers of the developing countries' primary exports appropriated the entire gain. That in practice we would expect the gain to be largely appropriated by the importers in the case of primary products which have price-inelastic demand does not of course imply that this outcome is distributionally just. (The developing countries cannot hope to make an off-setting gain on manufactured imports, if for no other reason than that transport costs constitute a much smaller proportion of total costs in manufactures than in primary products.)

4. THE QUALITY BIAS

In order to make a case that quality improvements were a source of bias which made the trend of the NBTT of primary products appear worse than it was, or even turned a real improvement into an apparent deterioration, it is necessary to show not only that quality improvements were under-allowed for in the price (unit value) index of manufactures but that they were more so than in the corresponding index for primary products. It has often been asserted but never demonstrated that this was and is the case. The argument was in fact all too readily granted by the UN document (UN 1949, pp. 120–1) which Prebisch used as his statistical source, and Prebisch himself (1950, p. 4) made a bow to the quality problem before passing on.

The problem of quality in the context of a price index has two facets: quality will improve if (i) the product mix alters in favour of higher quality goods within a group and (ii) technical progress imparts superior properties to a given good.

It is sometimes thought that primary products do not lend themselves to quality improvements, and this is true up to a point with respect to (ii). But the most cursory look at some facts will convince otherwise about (i). In Kenya the proportion of coffee beans of highest quality (AA) harvested in 1957–8 was 0.20 per cent; in 1964–5 it was 16.30 per cent (Krug and Poerck 1968, p. 133). In Greece 60.1 per cent of cotton output in 1954 had a staple length of 25mm or less and only 11.3 per cent of 28 mm or more; in 1970 the respective proportions were 0.1 per cent and 97.3 per cent (US Department of Agriculture 1971). In 1950 one-third of iron ores exported world-wide (but excluding intra-COMECON and intra-ECSC trade) had an Fe content of more than 60 per cent, but by 1964 more than half did (UN ECE 1968). Perhaps more important than any of these is the processing of primary products before shipment (for instance, cocoa beans turned into cocoa butter and cocoa paste) which has been increasing all the time, though in developing countries it has gained great momentum only in the last twenty years.

The obverse of the previous misapprehension is that manufactures are not subject to quality deterioration. But durability is one product characteristic, important to developing countries, with respect to which it is not self-evident that there hass been no deterioration.

If quality improvements are liable to be under-allowed for on both sides, no presumption can be established in the abstract regarding a systematic bias in terms of trade from this source. It is true that in arriving at the NBTT series set out in column (2) of Table III.1, the League (1945) used the Sauerbeck index for its price series of primary products, which index is constructed on the basis of prices for specific grades of commodities. Therefore no change of quality enters here at all. But the UN series of Table III.1, column (4) is based, in principle, on unit values on the side of both primary products and manufactures, and therefore biases would be occurring on both sides.

The conclusion is not that the NBTT series are free of quality bias; only that the alleged direction of the bias is a matter which cannot merely be asserted; it needs to be demonstrated.

Very tentatively an attempt could be made to go further by using the richer post-World War II data to throw 'experimental' light on the dark areas of the earlier record.

For primary commodities there exist parallel specific price and export unit value indices weighted by developing country exports — see, for example, World Bank (1976 and subsequent issues). As Kravis and Lipsey (1981) observe, there is no long-run divergence between the two which, on the face of it, is not consistent with a hypothesis of systematic quality improvement in primary commodities.

For manufactures, the data which bear on this point are less comprehensive due to the paucity of specific price indices. As reported in UN ECOSOC (1975), the US Bureau of Labor Statistics has experimented with specific price and unit value indices for manufactured exports in seven four-digit SITC classes. In three classes the unit value index went higher than the specific price index over a six-year period (1965-70), but in four it was the other way round. So, for manufactures too, no general support can be found for the proposition that the unit price index is subject to excessive inflation because it under-allows for quality improvements.

Kravis and Lipsey (1981) do infer some support for this proposition from the data that they assemble for developed country manufactured exports as a whole, but it is an unsustainable inference because virtually the entire difference between the unit value index and their specific price index over the period 1953-77 is concentrated in three years

(1972-5). To hypothesise a bunching of quality improvements as the source of this would be implausible.

So far then the experimental light does not expose a quality bias. But to take yet another step, some price indices of manufactures are explicitly adjusted for quality. The Federal Republic of Germany compiles both unit value and specific price indices for imports and exports, the specific price indices being based on a sample of 4000 goods and having quality adjustments as an integral part of the compilation in an attempt to arrive at a 'constant quality' price index. The comparison between the two indices for exports reveals that the unit value index rises more slowly throughout the seven years (1968-74) charted in the aforementioned ECOSOC paper. (But see Angerman (1980).) The same comparison for imports shows the two indices keeping in step for the first five years and then diverging in the last two in the same manner as for exports. At its face value this evidence again goes against the hypothesis that a unit value index is inflated by quality improvements. But once more Kravis and Lipsey (1981) draw a different inference from a quality-adjusted index of their own. This index rises more slowly than the unit value index with which they compare it, but the divergence is concentrated in the period 1953-64, which is the period with respect to which the coverage of their index is minimal.

Perhaps the only conclusion which can be derived at this point is that those who would deny the evidence of the NBTT series of Table III.1 on the ground of quality bias still have an onus to discharge.

Beyond all this, there is a fundamental question the answer to which may radically affect the perspective in which we view the quality bias: how do we assign the quality improvement of a manufactured article among the inputs? To take a simple example, is the quality improvement associated with bagged tea assignable to the tea or the bag or both? If we take away the bag most of the consumer's surplus remains, but if we take away the tea, none remains. So to exclude the tea from any share of the improvement does not seem plausible, at least in terms of this all-or-nothing test. For goods subject to a neoclassical production function we are not confined to an all-or-nothing test, but it is by no means obvious that zero is the proper share of quality improvements assignable to primary product inputs. So if, say, the natural rubber in quality-improved tyres which sell at an unchanged price can be said to have a share in the improvement, where does this leave the argument that the index of the terms of trade between primary products and manufactures is subject to a one-way quality bias?

5. WAS THE TIME SPAN OF THE STATISTICS CRITICAL?

Conclusions derived from time series are always subject to a question mark because of the unavoidable arbitrariness of the starting and finishing dates. The larger the series the lesser the problem. But, as Hagen (1968) and others have suggested, when the series ends in the 1930s it may be thought that there is still a problem given the dimensions of the slump at the time.

The crudest way of coping with this is to disregard the series after 1929. The bias imparted to the estimated deterioration by stopping at the cyclical peak of 1929 is an obvious objection against this procedure, though it should not be overstressed, because there is evidence that in the early 1870s primary product prices were also at a high level which, if true, gives rise to a counter-bias.

The Lewis index over the period 1871-1929 yields a trend rate of change of −0.28 per cent per annum (see row 4 of Table III.2) which, as expected, is lower than for the full period 1871-1938 but still a statistically significant deterioration.

A critic has pointed out that an anti-Prebisch position could be sustained nevertheless if Prebisch's own procedure of splicing two different series of the NBTT were adopted—in this case splicing Lewis's series for 1871-1900 and the UN's for 1900-29.[7] The resulting index number for 1929 is higher than for 1871. But note that such a result can be generated *only* when 1900 is used as the link year.

In order to avoid the arbitrariness of a particular link year we can compute time trends for the Lewis series 1871-99 and for the UN series 1900-29. As can be seen from rows 5 and 7 of Table III.2, the coefficient of t for the former is −0.55 per cent and for the latter statistically insignificant. Attaching the same weights to these results (since they relate to equal time spans), and given that there was no sharp discontinuity in the NBTT around the 1900 mark, the inference of overall deterioration for the two periods together is not altered, though clearly the change of trend as between the two periods is marked.

Another observation which points in the same direction is that, by the Chow test, the null hypothesis that the trend rates derived from the Lewis series 1900-29 and the UN series 1900-29 belong to the same statistical population is not rejected, and it is therefore implausible to draw any conclusions from combining Lewis 1871-1900 and UN 1900-29 which cannot be deduced from Lewis 1871-1929.

A rather more refined way of coping with cyclical influence on the time series is to introduce a cyclical demand variable in the regressions which will hopefully net out the cycle from the estimated trend. It so happens that Lewis (1952) complemented his NBTT series with an index of world production of manufactures (excluding the USSR). A semi-log trend line was fitted to the latter over the period 1871-1938 and the year-by-year residual from trend (D) was taken as the cyclical demand variable most appropriate to the purpose in hand. The Lewis series of Table III.1, column (3) was regressed on t and D and it can be seen (row 14, Table III.2) that the coefficient of t is −0.46 per cent. This is no different from the corresponding coefficient in the simple regression of the Lewis NBTT series on t alone (row 3, Table III.2), from which one may conclude that the deteriorating trend survives intact this way of removing the cyclical demand influence on the extremities of the NBTT series.

An alternative cyclical demand variable was also introduced—D' instead of D—which is the deviation from trend in Lewis's world production of manufactures series, but with the trend calculated over the period 1871-1929 only. As can be seen from row 15 of Table III.2, using D' does not affect the qualitative conclusion but reduces the coefficient of t to −0.29 per cent, or a deterioration of a little under one-third of one per cent per annum. The argument for adopting this procedure is that the Great Depression was so exceptional that it biased downwards the trend of manufacturing output. But now we have the opposite bias, since manufacturing output in 1929 was at a pronounced cyclical peak.

So the qualitative inference of deterioration survives decycling, but the rate of deterioration was smaller than Prebisch's statistics conveyed. This sums up the story so far. It is an open question whether there was much or little deterioration, but the statistical evidence is consistent with the view that there was some. In this weak form the conclusion is robust. This does not mean that it is the last word on the subject: if only because of the quality of the data, there cannot be a last word.

This part of the chapter is now complete. It must be viewed as an exercise in setting the record 'straight'. For this purpose the terms of reference were limited to the seventy-odd years down to World War II, the period over which the argument was initially joined.

6. WITH THE HINDSIGHT OF THE 1970s IS THERE A TREND?

Of course Prebisch, who initiated the debate, was not a mere observer of statistical history. He projected the deterioration into the future.

Since he first did this, time has elapsed and the pool of statistical evidence has expanded. Does the inference of deteriorating NBTT for primary products still survive? This is more subject to doubt.

The only remotely relevant year-by-year series which stretches for some decades on either side of World War II is that compiled by the UN and set out up to the year 1938 in Table III.1, column (4). It is continued for the post-World War II years in Table III.3, column (1*a*) (also in column (1*b*), rebased to 1960 = 100). Trend-fitting to this series over its whole length, 1900–70, yields a coefficient of t which is statistically insignificant (see row 8, Table III.2). A deteriorating trend is not now detectable.

For the post-World War II years, however, this is not the best series available. *Inter alia* it does not distinguish between primary products which are of major interest to developing countries and those which are not. It must therefore be tested against more appropriate series.

But first a warning about NBTT series which are sometimes used (for example MacLaren (1977)) but which are inappropriate. The series relating to aggregate merchandise imports and exports of developed market economy countries is totally inappropriate because it is heavily influenced by intra-trade of the group, which has the effect of pulling the index towards 100 since, with respect to such trade, favourable and unfavourable changes in the NBTT cancel out. Clearly such an index will be very sluggish and will not tell us much about relative price movement in the net trade between developed and developing countries, let alone between manufactures and primary products. The equivalent series for developing countries is better, because intra-trade is less important for this group, but still not very good. The practice of the UN *Statistical Yearbook* of confining its only Table labelled 'Terms of Trade' to 'gross' regional NBTT of this kind must bear some responsibility for the confused usage.

More appropriate NBTT series can be computed by using price indices published elsewhere in the UN *Statistical Yearbook*, but their coverage of the early 1950s is poor, and therefore preference has been given to the World Bank indices which are set out in Table III.3. They conform as closely as possible to the primary products/manufactures

TABLE III.3

Net barter terms of trade between primary products and manufactures since 1950

Price or unit value of primary products ÷ unit value of manufactures: 1960 = 100 (except column (1*a*))

	United Nations*		World Bank				UNCTAD§
			Market prices†			Unit values‡	
			1967–9 weights		1974–6 weights		
	(1)						
Year	(*a*) 1913 = 100	(*b*)	(2) including petroleum	(3) excluding petroleum	(4) excluding petroleum	(5) excluding petroleum	(6) excluding petroleum
1950	114	119	135	132	129	–	140
1951	118	123	123	132	130	–	143
1952	109	114	116	119	118	–	120
1953	109	114	121	115	114	–	116
1954	110	115	133	131	126	–	131
1955	106	110	129	125	123	–	128
1956	103	107	126	122	121	–	119
1957	103	107	119	112	114	–	110
1958	100	104	113	105	103	–	104
1959	98	102	106	104	102	–	101
1960	96	100	100	100	100	100	100
1961	93	97	96	94	94	94	91
1962	91	95	93	93	93	93	89
1963	93	97	94	96	99	95	93
1964	95	99	95	105	104	96	101
1965	91	95	94	106	101	95	99

1966	91	95	93	105	104	97	97
1967	88	92	89	97	96	96	90
1968	87	91	89	99	104	104	92
1969	86	90	89	101	110	109	97
1970	85	89	86	99	104	103	95
1971	–	–	89	88	90	89	84
1972	–	–	90	87	86	84	83
1973	–	–	112	112	106	93	104
1974	–	–	228	122	117	104	114
1975	–	–	204	89	84	87	82
1976	–	–	–	–	93	89	–
1977	–	–	–	–	104	94	–
1978					84		

Sources
Columns (1*a*) and (1*b*): UN, *Statistical Yearbook 1969* and UNCTAD, *Handbook of International Trade and Development Statistics 1972*.

Columns (2), (3), (4) and (5): International Bank for Reconstruction and Development, *Price Prospects for Major Primary Commodities*, Report Nos 814/76, 817/78 and 814/80, June 1976, June 1978 and January 1980, respectively.

Column (6): For the index of primary product prices, UNCTAD, *Handbook of International Trade and Development Statistics 1976*. For the index of unit values of manufactures, Report No. 814/76 cited above.

Notes to Table III.3
* Same as note 4, Table III.1. Column (1*a*) continues the series of column (4) of Table III.1. Column (1*b*) is the same as (1*a*) but with 1960 = 100.

† Indices of market-quoted prices of specific grades of primary commodities weighted by their shares in the exports of developing countries in the years 1967–9 for columns (2) and (3), and 1974–6 for column (4), divided by a unit value index pertaining to the total manufactured exports (for columns (2) and (3)) or to manufactures exported to developing countries (for column (4)) from developed market economies. Thirty-five primary commodities are included in column (2); the same minus petroleum in columns (3) and (4).

‡ Unit values for primary commodities and 1975 weights. Otherwise same as for column (4) in note †.

§ An UNCTAD index of market-quoted prices of primary commodities weighted by their shares in the exports of the developing countries in the years 1968–9 (but excluding exports under 'special arrangements' of bananas, rice and sugar) divided by the World Bank's unit value index for manufactures used in compiling the series of columns (2) and (3).

dichotomy, and the primary products are weighted according to their shares in developing country exports.[8]

Since the long-run UN index includes petroleum, its post-World War II segment (column (1*b*), Table III.3) is best tested by comparing it with the World Bank index which does the same (column (2) Table III.3. Visual inspection reveals that they are correlated, and this is confirmed by $R^2 = 0.88$. But a Chow test rejects the hypothesis that the trend rates implicit in the two series (see rows 9 and 10 of Table III.2) may be generated by the same statistical population. So, even if some of the difference is simply assignable to the more recent weights employed by the World Bank (which must inevitably lead to a more pronounced trend in a price index if there is a negative correlation between price and quantity) it could plausibly be argued that the UN index in the post-World War II years is not a good substitute for more appropriate series.

If in order to avail ourselves of the better statistics we resort to splicing the UN series (for pre-war) and the World Bank series of column (2), Table III.3 (for post-war) the arbitrariness in the choice of link year(s) will loom very large. It so happens, however, that even if we choose 1956 as the link, which is the most favourable to the deterioration hypothesis, the resulting hybrid series for the period 1900–70 yields a coefficient of t which is negative but not statistically significant at the 5 per cent level (see row 13 of Table III.2). Thus the conclusion of trendlessness for the period 1900–70 still stands. It is this evidence which led to the earlier statement that the survival of the inference of deteriorating NBTT is subject to doubt when the time span is extended to encompass the years since World War II.

The evidence is not, however, absolutely conclusive. A counter-case could be made along the following lines.

First, an alternative NBTT index since 1950, compiled by UNCTAD, is set out in column (6) of Table III.3 which suggests that the long-run UN index, regardless of whether it is taken straight or in the hybrid form just discussed, gives an over-optimistic picture of the relative price experience of the relevant primary commodities. This follows from a two-step comparison. By looking at the coefficients of t in rows 9 and 10 of Table III.2 it can be seen that the UN index shows a slower deterioration than the World Bank index inclusive of petroleum. This is the first step. The World Bank index exclusive of petroleum (column (3) Table III.3) shows, however, a slower deterioration than the UNCTAD index which also excludes petroleum: the respective coefficients of *t* are −1.1 and −1.6 per cent (see rows 11 and 12 of Table III.2). This is the second step; it leads directly to the opening sentence of this paragraph.

Second, the long-run UN index has been used as a starting-point to straddle World War II because it is the only one available on a year-by-year basis on both sides of the divide. There are, however, other indices for a few selected years, and they do not all tell the same story. One constructed by Yates (1959, p. 43) suggests that between his two pivotal dates, 1913 and 1953, the price of all primary exports relative to the price of manufactured exports (both regardless of origin but with the socialist countries of Eastern Europe excluded) declined by 12 per cent. This compares with a rise of 9 per cent shown by the UN index between these dates. A turnround such as this—of the order of one-fifth—can make a big difference to one's perception of reality. But granting some force to this point, let it be said on the other side that it is less applicable to the hybrid series, which has also been used to straddle World War II, because it stands halfway between Yates and the UN series in its estimate of the change between 1913 and 1953. Moreover, almost the entire difference between Yates and the UN series arises on the side of manufactures, the price of which Yates (1959) obtains by using Kindleberger's (1956) unit value estimates which were confined to industrial Europe—a practice which in this context means, in Yates's own words, that 'reliability declines steeply' (p. 218). And it should be added that a very different perception of reality is conveyed by Maizels (1963), whose story differs from that of the UN index by as much as Yates's but in the opposite direction.[9]

Third, by not going back further than 1900, the UN index is omitting the relative price decline of primary products which, according to the evidence of the other series, was so pronounced in the last quarter of the nineteenth century. Repair of this omission might not have been enough, by itself, to impart a declining trend to an otherwise trendless series, but would have added its influence in that direction. However, if this argument is to be used, it must not be overlooked that it is double-edged. For it is likely that by going further back into the nineteenth century it would be possible to find periods in relation to which the prices of primary products at the beginning of the twentieth century were higher, not lower.[10]

Fourth, if the high degree of resource utilisation and growth of output in developed countries in the post-World War II years down to the mid-1970s is considered unsustainable, a netting out of this factor's influence on primary product prices may change the perception that the raw statistics convey. The severe downturn of the NBTT of primary commodities in the early 1980s will contribute towards such a change of perception, though from a long run perspective it will be significant only if it is prolonged and not cyclical.

It is not intended to assess the combined weight of these points. It is perhaps impossible to do so satisfactorily. If somebody takes the view that they add up to a case for the persistence of deterioration in the relative price of primary exports of developing countries, he is entitled to this conclusion. (Such a conclusion requires of course that petroleum be excluded from the argument after its effective cartelisation in 1973.)

What has been said earlier in the present section places a question mark against this conclusion, it does not refute it. Apart from anything else, not all the facets of the problem revealed by the post-World War II data have been exhausted. As illustrations of complexities, which on the face of it do not make any significant difference but need bearing in mind, column (4) is added to Table III.3 to show the effects of changing the years from which weights are derived and of narrowing the developed country manufactured exports which enter the index to those destined for developing countries (and not to all destinations); column (5) is also added to show the difference it makes (mainly in the short run) when we switch from market prices to unit values for primary commodities. (Only marginal quantities of some commodities are exchanged at the prices quoted in commodity exchanges.)

7. CONCLUSION AND SUMMARY

From the perspective of the early 1980s and in the light of the relevant literature, there are two distinct questions which one may ask about the behaviour of the NBTT between primary exports of developing countries and manufactured exports of developed countries:

(a) what does the totality of the available record show?
(b) in the statistical debate initiated by Prebisch, which view accorded more with the facts over the specific historical period to which the debate initially related?

For the latter question the relevant period covers the seventy years down to World War II. Over this period the evidence points to a deteriorating trend in the relative price of primary products. Given the reservations which must be made about the quality of the evidence, there can be no finality about this conclusion, but it has been reached by examining one by one the main points adduced to question the inference of the deterioration and finding that they are contradicted or not confirmed by relevant material. The statistical series chosen by Prebisch did, however, exaggerate the rate of deterioration.

The essential difference between questions (a) and (b) is that the former does and the latter does not include the post-World War II years in its terms of reference. This is a big difference because, though the relative price of the developing countries' primary products has had its ups and downs since the war, it has on average done quite well by the standard of pre-war decades, even when petroleum is excluded (as a special case) since 1973. So, while the tendency for the NBTT to deteriorate cannot be decisively refuted, it is open to doubt when, as postulated in question (a), the record up to the 1970s is taken into account.

IV

FACTORIAL TERMS OF TRADE AS A MEASURE OF INEQUALISATION

The statistical evidence provides weak support for the hypothesis of deteriorating net barter terms of trade (NBTT). This much is clear from Chaper III when proper account is taken of both pre- and post-World War II evidence.

Moreover, the theoretical case for assigning welfare significance to changes in the NBTT is weak when factor productivity is changing. A deteriorating NBTT could be the consequence of favourable productivity growth, and to focus on the former only is therefore unsatisfactory.

It is perhaps unfortunate that the deterioration debate has revolved round the NBTT and no apologies are made for switching to an older tradition which assigns greatest significance to the doube factorial terms of trade (DFTT).

As documented in Chapter I, numerous authors have taken the view that in the thinking of classical economists the DFTT was the most important of the terms of trade concepts while in more recent writings on trade and development the DFTT has also been gaining ground.

Alongside the DFTT stands the concept of the single factorial terms of trade (SFTT). Though the latter plays a minimal part in this monograph, it will nevertheless be reviewed briefly in this chapter. The SFTT bear on a country's absolute welfare, while the DFTT bear on relative welfare between trading countries. Both narrow their vision to the sectors of the economy which produce exportables. The point of this is to isolate (even at the cost of neglecting some general equilibrium repercussions) the contribution of those sectors which are most directly influenced by international trade and specialisation.

For given tastes and internal income distribution, and for constant employment in the exportables-producing sectors, the welfare contribution of these sectors depends on their labour productivity and the terms on which exports exchange for imports. The factorial terms of trade capture both these components.

But, as traditionally formulated, they weight the components equally. It can easily be shown that this is a special case, albeit an important one which will play a crucial part in the chapters that follow.

Section 1 of this chapter is devoted to the point that the productivity component of factorial terms of trade must be labour productivity.

Section 2 explores the link between the SFTT and absolute real income per employed person, while section 3 switches to the relation between the DFTT and relative real income per employed person.

Section 4 adds an employment dimension to the factorial terms of trade, an extension which is important in the context of chronic unemployment.

Section 5 addresses the question of whether the welfare interpretation of trade indices is affected when one of the parties to trade is a substantial exporter of natural (exhaustible) resources.

In this chapter and in the monograph as a whole welfare is deemed to be positively associated with the size of a country's consumption basket or, in the more relevant relative version, with the size of the basket relatively to the trading partner's basket.

1. WHICH PRODUCTIVITY?

When the concept of factorial terms of trade was first launched, it was taken for granted that the relevant productivity was labour productivity, measured as output per person employed or per man-hour. Since then, the notion of total productivity (≡ output per weighted bundle of all factor imputs) has gained prominence. The few empirical studies of factorial terms of trade have followed a variety of practices. Devons (1954) and Kojima (1958) employed labour productivity, Appleyard (1974) mostly land productivity, Lerdau (1962) the productivity of an unspecified mix of inputs; while Lipsey (1963) estimated separately labour productivity and a combined labour and capital productivity.[1] But the case for preferring labour to total productivity in the present context is strong, not to say overwhelming.

Recall that we are interested in the factorial terms of trade as an indicator of changes in welfare which, abstracting from distribution, means changes of real income per head. We are not interested in real income per bundle of labour, land, physical capital, education, research and development, etc.

One of the pioneers of total factor productivity estimates viewed the growth of total productivity as 'some sort of measure of our ignorance about the cause of economic growth' (Abramovitz 1956). In this 'growth-accounting' view of productivity, the more we find out about the causes of growth the more the total factor productivity index will edge towards a zero rate of increase, paralleling a movement towards zero of the residual in time series-estimated aggregate production functions.[2] How far away this is from what is needed here can be illustrated by a simple example. Suppose the weather is included as an input and that it changes favourably, boosting agricultural output: the total productivity index will not change and the improvement in average income will be missed by such an index. The alternative view of a total productivity index is that to be of any use it must omit some of the relevant inputs for, as Domar (1962) put it: 'if we manage to identify *all* the "other forces", the measure of total productivity will never budge from unity and the index will be dead'. What inputs are then omitted or included is a matter which depends on the purpose in hand, and here it would serve no purpose to include any other input beside labour.

This is not to say that the growth of labour productivity should be conceived as costless. But the proper way of allowing for costs incurred (in the shape of capital formation and others) is to deduct from gross output that part which is not available for domestic consumption or export because it is needed to sustain the observed growth of labour productivity. As this is sometimes easier said than done, it should be added that there is a class of cases where it is not necessary—those where the proportion of gross investment to gross output stays roughly constant over the years. In these circumstances a gross labour productivity index (one which does not make allowances for capital formation) will behave in roughly the same way as a net index (one which does). Furthermore, when the home and foreign productivities enter as a ratio, as they do in the case of DFTT, the bias from not netting out capital formation is common to both numerator and denominator and thus to some extent self-cancelling.

2. SINGLE FACTORIAL TERMS OF TRADE

In the traditional version the SFTT are defined as

$$\text{SFTT} \equiv P\Pi_c, \qquad \text{(IV.1)}$$

where P stands for the price ratio between the exportable and the imported good (≡ net barter terms of trade) and Π_c for labour productivity in the home country's exportable.

Many tradable goods can be handled easily but there is a gain in expository convenience and no loss of generality in assuming just one exportable and one imported good. Production of non-exportables is not excluded but is of no concern here.

Logarithmic differentiation of (IV.1) yields

$$\frac{d(\text{SFTT})}{\text{SFTT}} \equiv \dot{\overbrace{\text{SFTT}}} = \dot{P} + \dot{\Pi}_c. \qquad \text{(IV.2)}$$

(The dots denote percentage changes in the neighbourhood of differentiation.) Thus, the percentage change of the SFTT decomposes into the unweighted sum of the percentage changes of relative price and productivity.

The SFTT are said to improve if (IV.2) is positive and deteriorate if negative. But the sum being unweighted means that improvement (deterioration) is neither necessary nor sufficient for a gain (loss) of welfare. Consider, for example, a situation in which a $\dot{\Pi}_c > 0$ is associated with a fall in the price of the exportable good such that $\dot{P} + \dot{\Pi}_c = 0$. The SFTT index will be unchanged but if some part of the exportable good is consumed at home, the price change relating to that part will constitute a redistribution between home producers and consumers and not an offset against the growth of productivity. There will thus be a net gain which the SFTT index will fail to register.

The appropriate weighting can be derived very simply. Let the price index be the geometric average of the exportable price (P_c) and the imported good price (P_m) : $P_c^{(1-\omega)}P_m^{\omega}$, where ω is the share of imports in the consumption basket. A geometric average is chosen because it is in keeping with the multiplicative character of factorial terms of trade. If E is money expenditure, then $E \div [P_c^{(1-\omega)}P_m^{\omega}]$ expresses expenditure in real terms. When trade is balanced[3] $E = P_cQ_c$, where Q_c is the output of the exportable. It follows that real expenditure = $P_cQ_c \div [P_c^{(1-\omega)}P_m^{\omega}] = [P_c/P_m]^{\omega}Q_c = P^{\omega}Q_c$. When employment is constant, as will be assumed until section 4, there is a one-to-one relation between an index of Q_c and an index of Π_c. Therefore, the index number of real expenditure per employed person ≡ weighted SFTT ≡

$$\text{WSFTT} = P^{\omega}\Pi_c. \qquad \text{(IV.3)}$$

Thus generalised, the formula acknowledges the fact that the terms of trade have no welfare implications for the non-exported fraction of exportable output.

The rate of change of the generalised index is

$$\overbrace{\text{WSFTT}}^{\bullet} = \omega\dot{P} + \dot{\Pi}_c. \tag{IV.4}$$

It reduces back to (2) when $\omega = 1$, a situation which would be approximated in economies which retain for home consumption a very small proportion of the exportables they produce (i.e. $1 - \omega \simeq 0$).

Typically the initial and terminal ωs will not be the same so here, as always, the standard index number problem raises its head.

Note in passing that if $\overbrace{\text{WSFTT}}^{\bullet} < 0$ as a result of $\dot{P} < 0$ which is attributable wholly to an exogenous $\dot{\Pi}_c > 0$, the weighted SFTT index would be registering what Bhagwati (1958, 1968 and numerous sequels) has called immiserizing growth.

3. DOUBLE FACTORIAL TERMS OF TRADE

The traditional definition of the DFTT is

$$\text{DFTT} \equiv P\frac{\Pi_c}{\Pi_m^*} \tag{IV.5}$$

where Π_m^* stands for labour productivity in the foreign country (rest of the world) exportable. (Hereafter in this chapter symbols which appertain to the foreign country will be asterisked.)

The rate of change of the DFTT is the sum of three unweighted terms:

$$\overbrace{\text{DFTT}}^{\bullet} = \dot{P} + \dot{\Pi}_c - \dot{\Pi}_m^*. \tag{IV.6}$$

How good an index of relative welfare is (IV.5)? To address this question assumes provisionally that each country produces one exportable good and nothing else.

On this assumption relative real income is given by $E/P_c^{(1-\omega)}P_m^{\omega} \div E^*/P_m^{(1-\omega^*)}P_c^{\omega^*}$. Bearing in mind that when trade is balanced $E = P_cQ_c$ and $E^* = P_mQ_m^*$, the expression for relative real income reduces to $(Q_c/Q_m^*)P^{\omega+\omega^*}$. Under the constant employment assumption (which is maintained until section 4), this converts to $kP^{\omega+\omega^*}\Pi_c/\Pi_m^*$, where k, being the (constant) ratio of persons employed in the respective countries, drops out when we view the last expression as an index number. We have in fact arrived at a weighted DFTT index:

$$\text{WDFTT} \equiv P^{\omega+\omega^*}\Pi_c/\Pi_m^*, \tag{IV.7}$$

the rate of change of which is now a weighted sum,

$$\overbrace{\text{WDFTT}}^{\bullet} \equiv (\omega + \omega^*)\dot{P} + \dot{\Pi}_c - \dot{\Pi}_m^*. \tag{IV.8}$$

The traditional unweighted version corresponds to the case where $\omega + \omega^* = 1$. This condition is satisfied when the two countries have identical consumption patterns, meaning that the two goods enter their consumption baskets in the same proportion.

In other cases the unweighted DFTT index overshoots or undershoots for two reasons. The first relates to the incommensurateness of the productivity and terms of trade effects. This is the same point as was noted in the context of the SFTT, only now productivities both at home and abroad enter the calculations. The second arises because the unweighted DFTT fail to acknowledge that the effect of a given price change on the relative real income of two countries is not independent of differences in their consumption patterns.

However, across the North/South divide the unweighted index may serve as a rough approximation in the context of major primary exportables of developing countries being traded against manufactures of developed countries. For products such as petroleum, coffee, cocoa, natural rubber, tin and some other non-ferrous metals, the proportion of output exported to developed countries (and hence the proportion of imports to that output) is in the range 70-90 per cent, while some 5-10 per cent of manufacturing production of developed countries goes to the developing countries. So $\omega + \omega^* = 1$ is not drastically violated.

Additionally, the unweighted DFTT are unbiased when P is trendless. This is trivially obvious but again important in the North/South context because, as was seen in Chapter III, the terms of trade between primary products as a group and manufactures seem to have been essentially trendless over the one-hundred-plus years since 1870 and, excluding petroleum, the same is true for the span of twenty-odd years since 1960, to which span much empirical work bearing on North/South economic relations has to be confined because of data poverty in earlier decades.

Two further points before concluding this section.

First, has the index in (IV.7) perhaps moved so far from a sense related to the terms of trade that continuing adherence to a terms of trade nomenclature cannot be justified? The unweighted DFTT represent the number of man-hours needed on average to produce foreign exportables of a value equal to one hour's production of home exportables. The terms of trade meaning of the WDFTT is an extension of that: it is the rate at which one home man-hour exchanges for foreign man-hours via the intermediation of trade, but with due regard for the importance of the traded goods in the respective consumption baskets. This carries the spirit of the DFTT to its logical conclusion: it represents an exchange ratio, which if maintained constant, would imply unchanged real income relativity between the home country and the rest of the world.

Second, what difference does it make if production of non-exportables is allowed for? If the total economies of the two countries are in scale to their exportables-producing sectors, there is no difference. If they are not in scale, changes in real income relativity between the two countries will depend not only on the components of (IV.8) but also on the proportions of non-exportables in their respective economies. This would either have to be allowed for separately, or it may be argued that if the object is to identify how the pattern of international specialisation has been contributing to welfare, this is properly done on an 'as if' basis—as if the total economies were proportional to the exportables-producing sectors.

4. EMPLOYMENT-CORRECTED FACTORIAL TERMS OF TRADE

Constant employment in exportables has been assumed hitherto.

This is a harmless assumption for an economy which has full employment and perfect mobility between exportables and non-exportables. The price-weighted marginal products of different sectors will then be equal and a change of employment in exportables would be offset by changes in other sectors and would affect neither the absolute real income of a country nor its relative income *vis-à-vis* the rest of the world.

But at the other extreme if there is a pool of chronically unemployed labour, or nominally employed labour but with zero marginal product, an increase of employment in exportables which draws on this pool would have the same effect on absolute and/or relative real income as an increase in productivity. One may wish to discriminate between them on social, distributional, or developmental grounds, but these are not relevant here. In such a case therefore employment and productivity must be treated symmetrically. The resulting index will be said to be 'employment-corrected'. For developing countries the employment-corrected version may be especially relevant.

The employment-corrected WSFTT (ECWSFTT) is given by

$$\text{ECWSFTT} \equiv P^{\omega}\Pi_c N_c \qquad \text{(IV.9)}$$

where N_c is an index of the volume of labour in exportables. $\Pi_c N_c$ now stands where Π_c alone stood before (compare expression (IV.3)) but nothing else changes and the welfare implications are unaffected since output is output for the present purposes regardless of how it is apportioned between employment and productivity.

In the case where $\omega = 1$, $\Pi_c N_c = X \equiv$ volume of exports, and (IV.9) reduces to what Dorrance (1949-50) christened the 'income terms of trade' (ITT):[4]

$$\text{ITT} \equiv PX.$$

Since $P \equiv P_c/P_m$ and $P_c\Pi_c N_c \equiv V_c \equiv$ value of output of exportables,

$$\text{ECWSFTT} \equiv \frac{P_c^{\omega-1}V_c}{P_m^{\omega}} \qquad \text{(IV.10)}$$

which is empirically convenient because reasonable proxies for V_c can be procured whereas for developing countries data for Π_c are much harder to obtain, at least for their agricultural exportables.

Turn now to the relative income index which is the main concern of this chapter. Let us consider it in the context of the North/South dichotomy taking it as a stylised fact that in the South (the home country) there is chronic unemployment while in the North there is full employment.

In this context the employment-corrected WDFTT index (ECWDFTT) will be affected asymmetrically, the home country's volume of employment entering the numerator but the foreign country's missing from the denominator:

$$\text{ECWDFTT} \equiv \frac{P^{\omega+\omega^*}\Pi_c N_c}{\Pi_m^*}$$

$$\equiv \frac{P_c^{\omega+\omega^*-1}V_c}{P_m^{\omega+\omega^*}\Pi_m^*}. \qquad \text{(IV.11)}$$

The index we now have charts relative welfare with due allowance for changes of employment where it matters.

When the total labour force (N) is not constant, the employment component of (IV.11) must be normalised:

$$\text{normalised ECWDFTT} \equiv \frac{P^{\omega+\omega^*}\Pi_c \dfrac{N_c}{N}}{\Pi_m^*} \qquad \text{(IV.12)}$$

An obvious extension will take care of chronic unemployment in the foreign country as well.

In North/South contexts, where $\omega + \omega^* = 1$ is empirically approximated, the unweighted version (ECDFTT) can be resorted to and advantage will be taken of this in the two succeeding chapters.

5. WELFARE IMPLICATIONS OF TRADE IN NATURAL RESOURCES

When natural resources are exchanged for reproducible goods, as happens across the developed/developing divide, the line between improvement and deterioration of welfare, be it relative or absolute, of the resource owner cannot lie at the point where any of the preceding indices are unchanged.

To see this we need to concentrate on the relative price (≡ NBTT) component of those indices. For this purpose assume that both employment and productivity are constant all round. To make things simple assume also that the natural resources are costlessly extractable.

Suppose now that at some initial year the revenue from exporting the entire volume of output extracted is consumed. If the NBTT are unchanged the following year, the purchasing power per unit of the resource is the same but the owners of the resource are worse off: they have consumed capital and this makes clear that they cannot sustain the preceding year's consumption standard indefinitely.

From their viewpoint, a welfare-neutral time path would be one which maintains their initial consumption level *and* keeps their capital intact. For this to happen the relative price of the resource must rise *at the same rate* as the stock of the resource is depleted. This will keep the value of capital intact. It will also maintain revenue per unit time unchanged when a constant fraction of the stock is extracted, since volume extracted will then fall at a rate equal to the depletion of the stock.

With an exogenously given interest rate, a competitive market will bring about this result if, but only if, the price elasticity of demand for the resource is unity. This can be seen intuitively as follows. In keeping with the central theorem of competitive natural resource pricing, first derived by Hotelling (1931) and endlessly repeated in recent years, the equilibrium price of the resource must rise at a rate equal to the interest rate. If it rose at a slower rate, resource owners would extract a larger amount today and invest the sales proceeds at the going interest rate. If it rose at a faster rate, they would keep the resource in the ground. With unity price elasticity, revenue will be constant and hence the capitalised value of the diminishing stock will also be constant at successive points of time.

If demand is inelastic, revenue will be rising and the capital value of the stock will also be on a rising path—and conversely if demand is elastic.[5]

The basic conclusion (which generalises to the case of positive costs of extraction, provided the pure royalty element of a resource price is non-negligible) is that welfare neutrality for a resource-owning country requires continuously improving NBTT.[6] Of course this is welfare diminishing for the resource-consuming country, for which the welfare-neutral point is still at constant NBTT. In the light of this we have to accept either a double standard of neutrality, one for the resource exporter and another for the resource importer, or we may argue that since resource exhaustion is a cost which must be borne by the world economy, an intermediate point between the two standards should serve as the welfare-neutral mark for both countries, which in the abstract is more appealing but the exact location of this mark will depend on burden-sharing weights which are ultimately subjective.

Since the NBTT are a component of both the SFTT and DFTT, in their case too constancy cannot be the borderline. Viewed from the standpoint of resource-exporting countries, staying on the borderline requires a positive trend.

6. CONCLUSION

The central purpose of this chapter was to establish exactly what factorial terms of trade measure. The attraction of the DFTT is that, as between two fully employed and fully specialised economies, they provide an index of relative income per head of the labour force. The DFTT serve therefore as a criterion of incremental (in)equalisation, i.e. (in)equalisation in comparison to some earlier position, not to a hypothetical no-trade alternative. In less than fully specialised economies they signpost the contribution towards incremental (in)equalisation being made by those sectors which are most directly influenced by international trade and specialisation. For greatest generality the DFTT index needs to be weighted, but it is serviceable in the traditional unweighted version for major cases of practical importance.

In less than fully employed economies the output implications of productivity growth and fuller employment are analogous, so the productivity and relative price dimensions of the DFTT must be augmented to encompass a third dimension—that of employment. This gives rise to what has been termed the employment-corrected DFTT and it is this which is quantified in Chapter VI.

V

MODELLING INEQUALISATION

The welfare economics of factorial terms of trade having been discussed in Chapter IV and their credentials as criteria of inequalisation having been examined, it is now time to turn to positive economics.

With the aid of a model which will start very simply and will then moderately escalate in complexity, the object will be to identify some forces which, in the North/South context, influence the movement of the double factorial terms of trade (DFTT) and of the employment-corrected DFTT (ECDFTT) and to enquire whether a presumption about their direction can be established. Observe that the unweighted versions of both the DFTT and ECDFTT are being used. These simplify the theory and, as noted in Chapter IV, they are not a serious embarrassment in important empirical contexts across the developed/developing divide.

The direction of the net barter terms of trade (NBTT) will also be examined for, if it is a fact (as the evidence of Chapter III suggests) that there has been no deterioration of the NBTT of primary products over the long run, a hypothesis of DFTT deterioration can only be viable if the conditions for it are less stringent than for NBTT deterioration.

Two facts will be taken for granted and are crucial to the analysis: income-inelastic and price-inelastic demand for primary products (always excluding petroleum).[1] For both there is emphatic empirical support.[2]

There will be two economies throughout, Southland and Northland. Product markets will always be assumed to clear. Initially both economies are fully employed and fully specialised, Southland in primary commodities and Northland in manufactures. Output changes only as productivity changes exogenously. This case lends itself to diagrammatic treatment. Given the elasticity assumption, it yields a presumption of DFTT deterioration for Southland's primary commodities and the conditions for such deterioration are unambiguously less stringent than for NBTT deterioration.

Next, chronic unemployment is introduced in Southland via a 'primitive' sector in which labour has a zero marginal product and from which labour can be drawn into commodity production. The presumption of DFTT deterioration is reinforced by this extension. But in the presence of unemployment greater interest attaches to the ECDFTT. For this too the model yields a presumption of deterioration.

The next and final extension of the model dilutes the presumption of deterioration. Incomplete specialisation in Northland is allowed for and Southland output of primary commodities can displace Northland output of the same. It now matters what Southland's share of 'world' primary production is and what the share of primary products in Northland's aggregate output is.

In relation to the real world developed/developing dichotomy, the last extension of the model has no relevance so far as tropical beverages, bananas, some non-ferrous metals, and other commodities overwhelmingly dominated by developing country production are concerned. The dilution of the deterioration presumption may therefore be deemed to be limited.

If so, inequalisation could be traced back to income and price inelasticities (together with a high share of world production for the major export commodities), a conclusion which, if unexciting, is appealing to common sense. To underpin (within a market-clearing framework) the developing world's dissatisfaction with the traditional pattern of trade it is not necessary to resort to assumptions which yield 'perversely' sloped excess supply functions, as, for example, in Chichilnisky (1981).

Of course, by itself, no amount of theoretical modelling can be conclusive. Complementary empirical evidence on inequalisation will be offered in the next chapter.

1. THE SIMPLEST MODEL

The model which serves as a starting-point is one which yields the most widely quoted formula in the literature for the direction of change of the NBTT in response to exogenous labour productivity growth—*inter alia* in Johnson (1955, 1959), Kemp (1955), Bhagwati (1958), Johnston and Tolley (1965), de Figueroa (1969), Lewis (1972), and Findlay (1981). This model permits the essential comparison between conditions for DFTT and NBTT deterioration to be made in the most familiar context. It also lends itself to simple theoretical extensions with intuitive appeal and easily observable empirical implications.

The production side of the model remains rudimentary throughout. But it is conceptually attuned to the factorial terms of trade framework. Treating productivity growth as exogenous acknowledges the fact that productivity-improving innovations are motivated by competition at the level of individual producers, thus being a microeconomic phenomenon which cannot be satisfactorily modelled macroeconomically.[3]

The two countries of the model specialise fully—Northland in manufactures and Southland in commodities. Commodities are assumed to be either reproducible (agricultural goods) or, if natural resources, indistinguishable from reproducible goods because their known or anticipated reserves are very large. This essentially excludes petroleum, which may in any case be excluded as a fully cartelised commodity.

The symbols will be defined as they are introduced but are also assembled in an appendix.

The rudimentary 'production functions' for the two goods are

$$S_c = \Pi_c N_c, \tag{V.1}$$

$$S_m^* = \Pi_m^* N_m^*, \tag{V.2}$$

where S is volume of output or supply, Π is a labour productivity measure which is governed by exogenous technical progress and N is the number of persons at work. The subscripts c and m assign the symbols to which they are attached to commodities and manufactures respectively. The asterisk denotes symbols pertaining to Northland.[4] It is assumed that for the time being $\dot{N}_i[\equiv dN_i/N_i] = 0$, but $\dot{\Pi}_i[\equiv d\Pi_i/\Pi_i] > 0$ $(i = c, m)$ throughout.

The demand functions are world-wide aggregates. The superscript g (for global) indicates this. For the sake of the accompanying diagrammatic illustration, the demand for commodities (D_c) and for manufactures (D_m) are viewed temporarily as a ratio:

$$\frac{D_c^g}{D_m^g} = \frac{D_c^g}{D_m^g}(P, Y_r^g) \tag{V.3}$$

where $P \equiv P_c/P_m \equiv$ NBTT and $Y_r \equiv$ real income, i.e. income measured at the initial price ratio $P(0)$, or more precisely

$$Y_r^g = S_m^* + P(0)S_c. \tag{V.4}$$

Given that (V.3) is a ratio of volumes demanded, its elasticity is a substitution elasticity (η_s^g), defined in the usual way:

$$\eta_s^g \equiv \frac{P\partial(D_c^g/D_m^g)}{(D_c^g/D_m^g)\partial P} < 0.$$

Price is determined by the market-clearing mechanism which is captured in the following equilibrium condition:

$$\frac{D_c^g}{D_m^g} = \frac{S_c}{S_m^*}. \qquad \text{(V.5)}$$

There is at this stage no asymmetry between Northland and Southland. That will come later. The Prebisch-type asymmetry, whereby the price of manufactures is monopolistically administered while the price of commodities is competitively determined, does not add anything of long-run significance (see Chapter II, section 1), since P is a price ratio and one cannot anchor a ratio by anchoring only one side of it. The model is compatible with a given degree of monopoly in the market for manufactures.

The diagram of Figure V.1 captures all the essential elements of this model. There is one D_c^g/D_m^g curve for each level of Y_r^g. As real income rises, thanks to productivity growth, the curve shifts to the left because the growth of demand is anti-commodity biased. This is the consequence of the fundamental assumption that the demand for commodities is income-inelastic ($\epsilon_c^g < 1$, whence it follows that $\epsilon_m^g > 1$).

The ratio S_c/S_m^* is independent of P, hence the corresponding curve is vertical but the curve shifts when $\dot{\Pi}_c \neq \dot{\Pi}_m^*$. In Figure V.1 the S_c/S_m^* curve is shifted arbitrarily to the left, indicating an anti-commodity bias in the growth of supply ($\dot{\Pi}_c < \dot{\Pi}_m^*$).

2. THE EFFECT ON THE NBTT AND THE DFTT

The NBTT ($\equiv P$) can be read directly from the vertical axis. The new equilibrium E_1 may be at a higher or lower P as compared with E_0. The relative shift of the curves is critical. If, as in Figure V.1, the anti-commodity bias of supply growth (leftward shift of the S_c/S_m^* curve) is greater than the anti-commodity bias of demand growth (leftward shift of the D_c^g/D_m^g curve), the NBTT of commodities will improve.

If, however, $\dot{\Pi}_c > \dot{\Pi}_m^*$, the S_c/S_m^* curve will shift to the right and the NBTT of commodities will necessarily deteriorate.

The precise formula which the model yields[5] is

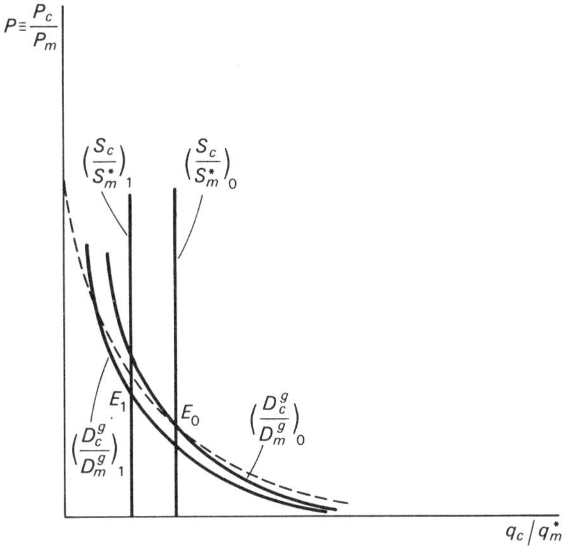

Figure V.1

$$\dot{P} \equiv \frac{dP}{P} = \left[-\frac{(1 - w_c^g \epsilon_c^g)}{1 - w_c^g}\, \dot{\Pi}_c + \epsilon_c^g \dot{\Pi}_m^* \right] \div -\eta_s^g, \tag{V.6}$$

where $\epsilon^g \equiv Y^g P \partial D^g / P D^g \partial Y^g > 0$ and $w_c^g \equiv P(0)D_c(0)/Y^g(0) \equiv$ initial weight of commodities in global output < 1.

Since $\eta_s^g < 0$, the sign of $\dot{P}$ will depend entirely on the sign of the square bracket in (V.6). Bearing in mind that the weighted sum of the income elasticities must equal unity, i.e. $w_c^g \epsilon_c^g + (1 - w_c^g)\epsilon_m^g \equiv 1$, this amounts to saying that the NBTT of commodities will improve or deteriorate according as

$$\frac{\epsilon_c^g}{\epsilon_m^g} \gtrless \frac{\dot{\Pi}_c}{\dot{\Pi}_m^*}, \tag{V.7}$$

which is the formula with the long pedigree that was referred to at the beginning of section 1 of this chapter and was also encountered in section 3(a) of Chapter II.

Turn now to the DFTT. By definition

$$\text{DFTT} \equiv P \frac{\Pi_c}{\Pi_m^*}. \tag{V.8}$$

To read on Figure V.1 the direction of change of the DFTT, we need the help of the broken curve which is drawn through E_0 and has a constant elasticity = 1, which means that $P(q_c/q_m^*)$ = constant at all points on the broken curve. $P(q_c/q_m^*)$ is the ratio of sales proceeds of commodities to sales proceeds of manufactures, which is synonymous with an index of sectoral income distribution and, when employment is constant in each sector, synonymous also with a DFTT index. Thus, a movement from a point on the broken line to a point above it implies an improvement of the DFTT of commodities, while a movement to a point below the broken curve implies a deterioration.

The D_c^g/D_m^g curves are drawn steeper than the broken curve in keeping with the assumption of price-inelastic demand for commodities.[6]

Consider now the case where $\dot{\Pi}_c < \dot{\Pi}_m^*$, which implies a shift of the S_c/S_m^* curve to the left. The associated increase of real income shifts the D_c^g/D_m^g curve to the left also, by virtue of the assumption that $\epsilon_c^g < 1$. As drawn in Figure V.1, the movement from E_0 to E_1 shows a deterioration in the DFTT of commodities, in contrast to the improvement of the NBTT. To get the DFTT to show an improvement at the same time as the NBTT, it needs a very large shift of the S_c/S_m^* curve relatively to the D_c^g/D_m^g curve. Thus an improvement of the DFTT is not impossible. It will occur if the supply growth of commodities is so slow relative to manufactures that, profiting from the price-inelastic demand for the former, it causes the relative price of commodities to rise by enough to compensate for their lagging productivity growth.

Unambiguously, however, the conditions for deterioration are less stringent for the DFTT than for the NBTT.

This may be confirmed by solving the model for a change in the DFTT. Differentiate (V.8) logarithmically to get

$$\overset{\bullet}{\overbrace{\text{DFTT}}} = \dot{P} + \dot{\Pi}_c - \dot{\Pi}_m^* \qquad \text{(V.9)}$$

[where $\overset{\bullet}{\overbrace{\text{DFTT}}} \equiv d(\text{DFTT})/\text{DFTT}$] and use (V.6) to substitute for $\dot{P}$ in (V.9):

$$\overset{\bullet}{\overbrace{\text{DFTT}}} = \left[-\frac{(1 - w_c^g \epsilon_c^g)}{1 - w_c^g} \dot{\Pi}_c + \epsilon_c^g \dot{\Pi}_m^* - \eta_s^g (\dot{\Pi}_c - \dot{\Pi}_m^*) \right] \div - \eta_s^g. \qquad \text{(V.10)}$$

The case of $\dot{\Pi}_c > \dot{\Pi}_m^*$ (rightward shift of the S_c/S_m^* curve) is not shown in Figure V.1, but it can readily be visualised that the DFTT for commodities will deteriorate.

3. RESTATEMENT AND FURTHER EXPLORATION

The relative demand function of (V.3) was diagrammatically convenient but otherwise awkward, particularly in compelling us to operate with a substitution elasticity. The model may therefore be restated more conventionally.

The place of (V.3) is taken by a demand function for commodities:

$$D_c^g = D_c^g(P, Y^g) \qquad (V.3')$$

where Y^g is income in terms of the numéraire (manufactures) and is subject to the identity

$$Y^g \equiv S_m^* + PS_c. \qquad (V.4')$$

The market-clearing condition is given by

$$S_c = D_c^g. \qquad (V.5')$$

By Walras's 'law', the market-clearing condition for manufactures is taken care of implicitly.

Adding equations (V.1) and (V.2), which may be used as they stand, completes the restatement. The model can be solved to yield an expression for $\overbrace{\text{DFTT}}^{\bullet}$ equivalent to (V.10) but now incorporating a Marshallian 'own price' elasticity for commodities

$$\left(\eta_c^g \equiv \frac{P\partial D_c^g}{D_c^g \partial P} < 0\right).$$

But instead of grinding out a solution *de novo*, there is a shortcut which may be used. When there are only two goods there is a strict relation (see Harberger (1957)) between the income-compensated Marshallian price elasticity ($\equiv \eta_c^g + w_c^g \epsilon_c^g$) and the income-compensated substitution elasticity (η_s^g) as follows:

$$\eta_c^g + w_c^g \epsilon_c^g \equiv (1 - w_c^g)\, \eta_s^g. \qquad (V.11)$$

By using (V.11) we can rewrite (V.10) as

$$\overbrace{\text{DFTT}}^{\bullet} = [-(1 + \eta_c^g)\dot{\Pi}_c + (\epsilon_c^g + \eta_c^g)\dot{\Pi}_m^*] \div -(\eta_c^g + w_c^g \epsilon_c^g), \qquad (V.10')$$

whence it can be seen that the DFTT of commodities will improve or deteriorate according as

$$\frac{\dot{\Pi}_c}{\dot{\Pi}_m^*}(1 + \eta_c^g) \lesseqgtr \epsilon_c^g + \eta_c^g. \qquad \text{(V.12)}$$

Deterioration is clearly the more plausible outcome. It can be established at sight that given ϵ_c^g, $|\eta_c^g| < 1$, the DFTT will deteriorate if $\dot{\Pi}_c \geqslant \dot{\Pi}_m^*$. If $\dot{\Pi}_c < \dot{\Pi}_m^*$, deterioration will occur if $1 > |\eta_c^g| \geqslant \epsilon_c^g$. But there may be non-deterioration when $\dot{\Pi}_c < \dot{\Pi}_m^*$ and $|\eta_c^g| < \epsilon_c^g$.

To explore further the circumstances of non-deterioration the 'matrix' of Table V.1 is computed from (V.12). Each cell gives the rate of relative productivity growth ($\dot{\Pi}_c/\dot{\Pi}_m^*$) which if not equalled or exceeded will yield non-deterioration of the DFTT, given the income and price elasticities listed at the head of the row and column of the chosen cell. For example, with $\epsilon_c^g = 0.7$ and $\eta_c^g = -0.4$, the growth of productivity in commodities must not be equal to or higher than half that of manufactures.

Cells to the south-west of the principal diagonal are blank because negative values of $\dot{\Pi}_c/\dot{\Pi}_m^*$ are excluded by assumption. The cells at or near the north-east corner of the matrix are almost certainly inadmissible because the combination of high ϵ_c^g and low η_c^g is liable to violate the condition derivable from the Slutsky equation that η_c^g must differ from 0 by an amount at least equal to $-w_c^g \epsilon_c^g$.

If, additionally, the first two rows and last two columns are neglected because they involve implausibly low price elasticities and implausibly high income elasticities respectively, we are left with the conclusion that DFTT deterioration will occur unless productivity growth in commodities is drastically slower than that in manufactures.

Against this background it is possible to view the hankering of primary-producing countries for cartelisation not as a means of attaining a distributive gain but of offsetting a growing distributive loss. Cartel-enforced restrictions of supply can counteract the growth of productivity and thus limit or reverse the damage done by productivity growth. For in the context of income and price inelasticity, the growth of supply associated with productivity growth is indeed damaging. As Robinson (1979, p. 68) and others have noted, there is a clear conflict between the private benefit from productivity growth accruing to an individual primary producer and the social loss inflicted on the totality of primary producers by the competition-induced drive for increased productivity.

TABLE V.1

Matrix of values of $\dot{\Pi}_c/\dot{\Pi}^*_m$ which if not equalled or exceeded will yield non-deterioration of the DFTT of commodities for selected values of ϵ^g_c and η^g_c.

η^g_c \ ϵ^g_c	0.1	0.2	0.3	0.4	0.5	0.6	0.7	0.8	0.9
−0.1	0.00	0.11	0.22	0.33	0.44	0.55	0.66	0.77	0.88
−0.2		0.00	0.125	0.25	0.375	0.50	0.625	0.75	0.875
−0.3			0.00	0.142	0.285	0.428	0.571	0.714	0.857
−0.4				0.00	0.166	0.333	0.50	0.666	0.333
−0.5					0.00	0.20	0.40	0.60	0.80
−0.6						0.00	0.25	0.50	0.75
−0.7							0.00	0.333	0.666
−0.8								0.00	0.50
−0.9									0.00

Of course the model which serves as background for these observations is a very simple one. The next step is to introduce some significant complications.

4. FIRST EXTENSION OF THE MODEL: ASYMMETRY WITH RESPECT TO UNEMPLOYMENT

The 'duality' of developing economies is captured in the hypothesis that in addition to their modern sector, to which the production of the major exportables may be deemed to belong, they have a primitive sector where there is effective unemployment in the sense that the marginal product of labour is zero—a hypothesis best known in the special case associated with the name of Lewis (1953) of 'unlimited supplies of labour' to the modern sector at a given real wage.

The unemployment of developed economies may be viewed as cyclical, not chronic, and for present purposes will be neglected. Asymmetry with respect to unemployment is often emphasised when structural characteristics of developed and developing countries are contrasted.

So, in terms of the model, Southland's *C*-producing sector can now draw on the labour pool of its primitive sector so that the labour supply function for the former sector is

$$N_c = N_c(P\Pi_c). \tag{V.13}$$

$P\Pi_c$ is income per person engaged in the commodity-producing sector, or average product of labour.[7] (V.13) is in keeping with the revenue-sharing hypothesis of wage determination but those who insist that labour is paid in proportion to its marginal product need not cavil at (V.13), because in a variety of plausible contexts the average and marginal products of labour grow proportionately, so that one serves as an index of the other. (Heady (1981) discriminates empirically between the two hypotheses and finds some support for both, but more for the former.)

The elasticity of labour supply implicit in (V.13) is $\nu_c \equiv P\Pi_c \partial N_c / N_c \partial (P\Pi_c) > 0$. It need not be infinite, as in Lewis (1953), even if mobility is perfect. Take the case where the total labour force in Southland ($\equiv N$) is constant. As N_c increases, N-N_c decreases and thus average income in the traditional sector rises, so that an increase in the average income of the commodity-producing sector will induce only a finite movement of labour. ν_c will then be restricted to

$\leqslant N\text{-}N_c/N_c$.[8] The Lewis case of infinite labour supply elasticity evidently arises when the modern sector is very small ($N_c \approx 0$).

The extended model comprises equation (V.13) in addition to equations (V.1), (V.2), (V.3′), (V.4′) and (V.5′) which have served before. (The primitive sector is presumed self-contained and its output can be left out of world income—equation (V.4′)—because it is constant by virtue of the zero marginal product assumption.) Differentiating logarithmically the equations of the model, solving for $\dot{P}$ and plugging the solution in (V.9) yields

$$\dot{\widehat{\mathrm{DFTT}}} = [-(1+\eta_c^g)\dot{\Pi}_c + (\epsilon_c^g + \eta_c^g)\dot{\Pi}_m^* - \nu_c(1 - w_c^g\epsilon_c^g)\dot{\Pi}_m^*] \div$$

$$\div [-(\eta_c^g + w_c^g\epsilon_c^g) + \nu_c(1 - w_c^g\epsilon_c^g)]. \qquad \text{(V.14)}$$

The denominator is unambiguously positive while the numerator has three terms of which the first two are the same as in (V.10′). Given the assumption that $\dot{\Pi}_m^* > 0$—together with $\dot{\Pi}_c > 0$ this is an assumption that is maintained throughout—the third term is unambiguously negative.

In other words, unsurprisingly, the pressure of excess labour makes the presumption of DFTT deterioration stronger. The logic is straightforward. As can be seen from (V.9), at constant DFTT, $d(P\Pi_c) > 0$ given $\dot{\Pi}_m^* > 0$. A rise in $P\Pi_c$ will attract labour to the C-producing sector which will exert a depressing influence on P, and therefore a more favourable constellation of circumstances than in the absence of excess labour will be required to sustain non-deterioration of the DFTT.

5. EMPLOYMENT-CORRECTED DFTT

The strengthening of the deterioration presumption for the DFTT of C-producers goes hand in hand, however, with a weakening of its welfare meaning for Southland. This is because the deterioration attributable to pressure of labour supply is accompanied by an increase in employment of hitherto unproductively occupied persons.

To tackle this problem the concept of the DFTT was widened in Chapter IV to allow for the employment dimension. This led to the concept of the employment-corrected DFTT defined as follows:

$$\mathrm{ECDFTT} \equiv \frac{P\Pi_c N_c}{\Pi_m^*}. \qquad \text{(V.15)}$$

The fact that only Southland labour enters the formula reflects the asymmetric assumptions about employment. Even if a second sector was introduced in Northland (as it will be in the next section), changes of employment in the *M*-producing sector, in so far as they reflect, in a full employment context, the switching of labour between sectors, would have a negligible effect on real income when high mobility equalises the price-weighted labour productivity across sectors.

It stands to reason that since, unlike the DFTT, the ECDFTT allow credit for *C*-output attributable to more employment, the condition for deterioration of the ECDFTT will be more stringent than for the DFTT.

Differentiating logarithmically (V.15) and using (V.13):

$$\overbrace{\text{ECDFTT}}^{\bullet} = (1 + \nu_c)\left(\dot{P} + \dot{\Pi}_c - \dot{\Pi}_m^* + \frac{\nu_c}{1 + \nu_c}\,\Pi_m^*\right) \qquad \text{(V.16)}$$

where $\overbrace{\text{ECDFTT}}^{\bullet} \equiv d(\text{ECDFTT})/\text{ECDFTT}$. Since $\dot{P} + \dot{\Pi}_c - \dot{\Pi}_m^* = \overbrace{\text{DFTT}}^{\bullet}$, it is evident that given $\dot{\Pi}_m^* > 0$, the ECDFTT may improve when the DFTT deteriorate but not vice versa.[9]

The precise condition for deterioration/improvement of the ECDFTT can be obtained by using (V.14) to substitute for $\dot{P} + \dot{\Pi}_c + \dot{\Pi}_m^*$ in (V.16). This yields

$$\overbrace{\text{ECDFTT}}^{\bullet} = \left[-(1+\eta_c^g)\dot{\Pi}_c + (e_c^g + \eta_c^g)\dot{\Pi}_m^* - (1+\eta_c^g)\frac{\nu_c}{1+\nu_c}\dot{\Pi}_m^*\right](1+\nu_c) \div$$
$$\div\,[-(\eta_c^g + w_c^g e_c^g) + \nu_c(1 - w_c^g e_c^g)]\,. \qquad \text{(V.17)}$$

The first two terms of the numerator remain the same as in (V.14) but the sign of the third now depends on the magnitude of η_c^g. But since it is taken as a stylised empirical fact that the demand for commodities is price-inelastic, the third term, which reflects the pressure of excess labour, contributes towards deterioration of the ECDFTT: the extra output from additional employment in *C*-making is more than offset by the resulting fall in price when demand is price-inelastic.

At the same time, the earlier assertion that the condition for ECDFTT deterioration is more stringent than that for DFTT deterioration is borne out by the fact that the third term in (V.17), if negative, is numerically smaller than the third term in (V.14).

Overall, the presumption from the model so far is that Southland's ECDFTT would deteriorate. As regards the first two terms of (V.17), the presumption established in section 4 is that their sum would be negative, and the addition of a third trerm which is negative when $\eta_c^g > -1$ strengthens the presumption of deterioration.

It is a critical feature of the model up to this point that Northland does not produce close substitutes for Southland's exportables. This is a fair representation of the real world in the case of the tropical beverages, some non-ferrous metals, and a few other commodities, which in total account for over a quarter of the developing world's non-fuel primary exports. To represent the rest, the model must be extended further.

6. SECOND EXTENSION: INCOMPLETE SPECIALISATION

By introducing, as the next step, a second sector in Northland, which produces substitutes for the imported commodities, the stage is set for a mechanism which counteracts the tendency towards deterioration of Southland's ECDFTT by giving Southland's exportables the opportunity to displace Northland output.

To give this mechanism maximum scope it will be assumed that the substitutes are perfect (same good), that mobility between sectors in Northland is perfect and that no protectionist measures are triggered off by an influx of imports. These are extreme assumptions so in contemplating the results of the model due regard will have to be paid to their extremeness.

Northland's labour force continues to be fully employed but it can now move between the *M*- and *C*-producing sectors. Labour supply to the *C*-producing sector will depend on relative earnings which are assumed to be related to price-weighted relative productivities. In symbols

$$N_c^* = N_c^*\left(\frac{P\Pi_c^*}{\Pi_m^*}\right). \tag{V.18}$$

It will be assumed that the elasticity of (V.18) (denoted by ν_c^*) $= \infty$, which means that mobility in Northland is perfect, unlike Southland where perfect mobility may be viewed only as a limiting case. This captures the widespread notion that material incentives work powerfully in developed market economies but typically less so in developing ones. The effect is that, in equilibrium, earnings in Northland's two sectors are equal. This enhances the asymmetry between Northland and Southland. In the latter, the opportunity cost of an increment of the modern sector's primary commodities is zero; in the former, an addition to the output of one sector is exactly matched (when price weighted) by foregone output in the other.

But at this point a symmetry which is normally not emphasised will be introduced. As in Southland's primitive sector, output per person engaged in Northland's primary sector will be taken to rise as numbers engaged in that sector fall. This could be accounted for by diminishing returns to land for a given organisation of the primary sector's production but is more accurately, and in the context of the model more conveniently, viewed as resulting from the substantial streamlining of agricultural organisation which is made possible by the reduction in the number of farming units. Auer (1969) estimates that nearly half of the dramatic productivity growth in US and Canadian farming over the period 1947-65 is attributable to the efficiency-promoting effects of a diminishing labour force.

Thus Π_c^* may now be viewed as having an autonomous component ($\tilde{\Pi}_c^*$) and a component inversely related by an elasticity coefficient (β) to the size of the labour force (N_c^*):

$$\Pi_c^* = \tilde{\Pi}_c^* N_c^{*-\beta} \quad (\beta > 0 \text{ and, to exclude instability,} < 1). \qquad \text{(V.19)}$$

Using (V.19) we can rewrite (V.18) as

$$N_c^* = \phi \left[\frac{P\tilde{\Pi}_c^*}{\Pi_m^*} \right] \qquad \text{(V.20)}$$

the elasticity of which $= 1/\beta$ when mobility is perfect.[10]

Π_m^* and Π_c continue to grow just exogenously. It will be arbitrarily assumed that $\tilde{\Pi}_c^* = \alpha \Pi_c$ (α = constant), so that the exogenous productivity growth rate is equal in the primary sectors of the two countries (i.e. $\dot{\tilde{\Pi}}_c^* = \dot{\Pi}_c$). Via this assumption (V.20) becomes

$$N_c^* = \phi \left[\alpha \frac{P\Pi_c}{\Pi_m^*} \right] \qquad \text{(V.21)}$$

with an elasticity still $= 1/\beta$ but with the great convenience that we now have the DFTT as the relevant independent variable.

The rest of the model can be dealt with rapidly.

Given a constant and fully employed labour force in Northland ($\bar{N}^*$), the labour supply in manufacturing is given by

$$N_m^* = \bar{N}^* - N_c^*. \qquad \text{(V.22)}$$

The global supply of commodities is

$$S_c^g = \Pi_c N_c + \Pi_c^* N_c^*$$

which, on the aforesaid assumptions, may be written as

$$S_c^g = \Pi_c N_c + \alpha \Pi_c N_c^{*(1-\beta)}, \qquad \text{(V.23)}$$

while the world supply of manufactures is as before

$$S_m^* = \Pi_m^* N_m^*. \qquad \text{(V.2')}$$

The global demand function for commodities remains unchanged,

$$D_c^g = D_c^g(P, Y^g), \qquad \text{(V.3')}$$

while the definition of global income (excluding a presumed self-contained primitive sector in Southland)

$$Y^g \equiv S_m^* + PS_c^g \qquad \text{(V.24)}$$

and the market-clearing condition for commodities

$$S_c^g = D_c^g \qquad \text{(V.25)}$$

are modified only marginally. The market for manufactures is cleared implicitly by Walras's law.

Equations (V.21), (V.22), (V.23), (V.2′), (V.3′), (V.24), and (V.25) together with equation (V.13) from section 4 constitute a complete model which, after logarithmic differentiation, can be written as shown overleaf in (V.26).

To take a passing glance at the DFTT in the new context solve this system for $\dot{P}$ and substitute into (V.9) to get

$$\overbrace{\text{DFTT}}^{\cdot} = \left[-(1+\eta_c^g)\dot{\Pi}_c + (\epsilon_c^g + \eta_c^g)\dot{\Pi}_m^* - \frac{S_c}{S_c^g} v_c (1 - w_c^g \epsilon_c^g)\dot{\Pi}_m^* \right] \div \Delta. \qquad \text{(V.27)}$$

Δ is the determinant of the matrix in (V.26) and is unambiguously positive.[11]

The numerator of (V.27) differs insignificantly from that of (V.14), hence the conclusion that the pressure of excess labour strengthens the presumption of DFTT deterioration carries over intact in the more extended model. Intersectoral mobility of labour in Northland does not affect the direction (though it affects the magnitude) of the DFTT because it is itself triggered off by a change of the DFTT—see (V.21).[12]

The main interest is in the ECDFTT. By using (V.27) to substitute for $\dot{P} + \dot{\Pi}_c - \dot{\Pi}_m^*$ in (V.16) we obtain

$$
\begin{bmatrix}
1 & 0 & 0 & -\nu_c & 0 & 0 & 0 & 0 \\
0 & 1 & 0 & -1/\beta & 0 & 0 & 0 & 0 \\
0 & N_c^*/N_m^* & 1 & 0 & 0 & 0 & 0 & 0 \\
-S_c/S_c^g & -(S_c^*/S_c^g)(1-\beta) & 0 & 0 & 1 & 0 & 0 & 0 \\
0 & 0 & -1 & 0 & 0 & 1 & 0 & 0 \\
0 & 0 & 0 & -\eta_c^g & 0 & 0 & 1 & -\epsilon_c^g \\
0 & 0 & 0 & -w_c^g & -w_c^g & -(1-w_c^g) & 0 & 1 \\
0 & 0 & 0 & 0 & 1 & 0 & -1 & 0
\end{bmatrix}
\begin{bmatrix}
\dot{N}_c \\ \dot{N}_c^* \\ \dot{N}_m^* \\ \dot{P} \\ \dot{S}_c^g \\ \dot{S}_m^* \\ \dot{D}_c^g \\ \dot{Y}^g
\end{bmatrix}
=
\begin{bmatrix}
\nu_c \dot{\Pi}_c \\ (1/\beta)(\dot{\Pi}_c - \dot{\Pi}_m^*) \\ 0 \\ \dot{\Pi}_c \\ \dot{\Pi}_m^* \\ 0 \\ 0 \\ 0
\end{bmatrix}
\qquad \text{(V.26)}
$$

$$\widehat{\text{ECDFTT}} = \Bigg[-(1+\eta_c^g)\dot{\Pi}_c + (\epsilon_c^g + \eta_c^g)\dot{\Pi}_m^* - $$

$$- (1+\eta_c^g)\frac{\nu_c}{1+\nu_c}\dot{\Pi}_m^* + \frac{S_c^*}{S_c^g}(1 - w_c^g\epsilon_c^g)\frac{\nu_c}{1+\nu_c}\dot{\Pi}_m^* +$$

$$+ \frac{S_c^*}{S_c^g}\left(\frac{1-\beta}{\beta}\right)(1 - w_c^g\epsilon_c^g)\frac{\nu_c}{1+\nu_c}\dot{\Pi}_m^* +$$

$$+ \frac{N_c^*}{N_m^*}\left(\frac{1}{\beta}\right)\epsilon_c^g(1 - w_c^g)\frac{\nu_c}{1+\nu_c}\dot{\Pi}_m^* \Bigg] \frac{1+\nu_c}{\Delta}. \qquad \text{(V.28)}$$

The mysteries of this complicated expression can be easily unravelled. The first two terms have been with us since section 3, where it was established that their sum may be presumed negative. The third term, which reflects the pressure of excess labour, first appeared in expression (V.17) and is negative when, as assumed, $\eta_c^g > -1$.

The remaining terms in the square bracket are new and stem from the presence of a *C*-producing sector in Northland (fourth term) and the intersectoral movements of labour which are now possible there (fifth and sixth terms).

The fourth term must be paired with the third. It will be recalled that the third term pushes the ECDFTT towards deterioration when $\eta_c^g > -1$ because the expansion of employment is more than offset by the fall in price. But when some part of *C*-output is produced in Northland, the burden of the price fall on that part is not borne by Southland and $\eta_c^g > -1$ is no longer enough for Southland's excess labour to have adverse effects on its ECDFTT. The extent to which it is not enough is governed by the fourth term which is $\geqslant 0$. In the limiting case where there is no *C*-production in Northland, $S_c^*/S_c^g = 0$ and the fourth term vanishes.

The fifth term is again $\geqslant 0$ and represents the replacement of primary production in Northland by employment-enhancing and hence ECDFTT-improving primary production in Southland. This occurs because at the borderline where $\widehat{\dot{\text{ECDFTT}}} = 0$ there must be a deterioration of the DFTT (see expression (V.16)), which means that there will be an incentive for Northland labour to move from the primary to the manufacturing sector. Note that the fifth term vanishes when $\beta = 1$. This is because the exodus of Northland labour from the primary sector is exactly compensated by the rise in the productivity of those who stay behind and there is no vacuum to be filled by expansion of Southland's primary production.

The sixth term is also $\geqslant 0$ and captures the effects of increasing world income arising from the intersectoral transfer of labour in Northland. Income increases (despite the fact that perfect mobility equalises incomes across sectors) as a result of the endogenous productivity element in the primary sector. It is best seen in the case where $\beta = 1$. In that case the primary sector's output does not fall as labour moves out, while the manufacturing sector's output rises as labour moves in. The increased income raises demand for commodities and generates employment for Southland labour.

7. A PRESUMPTION OF DETERIORATION

We have now allowed full play to the anti-deterioration mechanism inherent in Northland's incomplete specialisation. The balance between the pro- and anti-deterioration forces cannot be confidently predicted and, as in all interesting problems, it is a matter on which empirical evidence must be brought to bear. But there are pointers which help us to form a semi-*a priori* view about the direction of the ECDFTT and it is important that they be considered because, in a world of data mining, untested proxies, and error-prone data, statistical/econometric evidence does not by itself shed an undisputed light.

The first and most important pointer is that the anti-deterioration forces do not come into play at all for commodities such as cocoa, coffee, tea, bananas and tin, which account for over 25 per cent of developing country non-fuel primary exports and which have next to no close substitutes produced in developed countries. The remaining primary commodities are subject to both anti- and pro-deterioration influences, but the large component of the total which is subject only to the latter is liable to tilt the balance in the direction of deterioration.

Next it may be noted that in the model the cards have been stacked heavily towards anti-deterioration by the extreme assumptions that imported commodities have completely free entry into Northland and that Northland's domestic substitutes, where there are such, are perfect substitutes. But, of course, artificial fibres are not anywhere near perfect substitutes for cotton, synthetic rubber even less so for natural, and sugar imports are kept out of developed countries by automatically adjusting barriers (in the case of the EEC) of awesome efficiency. When the extreme assumptions are watered down the anti-deterioration forces are weakened.

Lastly, of the magnitudes on which the strength of the anti-deterioration mechanism depends, N_c^*/N_m^* is very small in the real world of developed countries, not just because labour engaged in primary production is only a small fraction of that engaged in manufacturing, but also because labour engaged in the production of non-competing primary commodities (in effect the bulk of temperate zone agriculture) must be excluded from N_c^*. β influences the result inversely: the larger it is, the smaller the anti-deterioration force. Calculations made by Auer (1969) imply roughly that $\beta = 5/6$ in the US and $= 2/3$ in Canada over the period 1947-65. The S_c^*/S_c^g ratio must be closer to zero than one, but is sensitive to choices about what to include or exclude in moving from the model to the real world. For example, while temperate agricultural products must clearly be excluded from the numerator, should the primitive sector's output in developing countries stay in or out of the denominator?

Such observations can never be conclusive but they cast doubt on the strength of the anti-deterioration force; it is more plausible to expect that it would be dominated than that it would dominate.

But note that the model implies that S_c/S_c^g will be rising over time while S_c^*/S_c^g and N_c^*/N_m^* will be falling—and the observed historical pattern across the developed/developing divide conforms with this. Two points follow. The first is that things will get worse rather than better if Southland stays with its traditional specialisation. The second is that if the empirical evidence confirms the deterioration presumption for recent years, it would not follow that the ECDFTT of developing countries have always been deteriorating. This is all the more so when it is borne in mind that the developing countries' main primary products must have had higher income and/or price elasticities in earlier phases of their life-cycle. Inequalisation, if present, is thus incremental; it occurs beyond a certain point.

8. CONCLUSION

In this chapter a first attempt has been made at theorising about relatively immiserising growth, as incremental inequalisation may be alternatively called. Although the issue has been much more prominent on the North/South agenda than absolutely immiserising growth, only the latter has been subjected to formal theorising hitherto—see

Bhagwati (1957-8, 1968 and numerous sequels) and for antecedents Bloomfield (1981).

The direction of the employment-corrected DFTT—the three-dimensional criterion of inequalisation developed in Chapter IV—has been examined in models of successively greater complexity. While abstract theorising cannot lead to an unambiguous conclusion, it is clear that unusual assumptions or implausible parametric values are not needed to yield at least a moderate presumption of inequalisation. The burden can be borne by income and price inelasticity of demand, than which nothing can be more commonplace in the context of the developing countries' traditional exportables.

Appendix: list of symbols

c	≡ Subscript attached to symbols pertaining to primary commodities.
D	≡ Demand.
DFTT	≡ Double factorial terms of trade.
ECDFTT	≡ Employment-corrected double factorial terms of trade.
g	≡ Superscript attached to symbols which refer to global aggregates.
K	≡ Capital.
m	≡ Subscript attached to symbols pertaining to manufactures.
N	≡ Employment (when without subscript it refers to total labour force in a country).
NBTT	≡ Net barter terms of trade.
P	≡ Price (without subscript $\equiv P_c/P_m$).
Q	≡ Volume of output of Southland's traditional sector.
r	≡ Subscript which distinguishes real income measured at constant prices from (unsubscripted) income at current prices.
R	≡ Ratio of average earnings in Southland's two sectors.
S	≡ Supply.
w	≡ Initial weight of a good in total output.
Y	≡ Income.
β	≡ Coefficient linking productivity to size of labour force in Northland's commodity-producing sector.
ϵ	≡ Income elasticity.
η_c	≡ 'Own price' elasticity of demand for commodities.
η_s	≡ Substitution elasticity between commodities and manufactures.

θ	$\equiv$ Measure of technical progress.
ν	$\equiv$ Elasticity of labour supply to commodity-producing sector.
Π	$\equiv$ Productivity.
ω	$\equiv$ Share of imports in consumption basket.
*	$\equiv$ Superscript attached to symbols pertaining to Northland. Southland symbols carry no superscript.
•	$\equiv$ Denotes percentage change of variable to which it is attached.

VI

DOCUMENTING INEQUALISATION THROUGH THREE-DIMENSIONAL FACTORIAL TERMS OF TRADE INDICES

In this chapter an attempt is made to cover with empirical flesh the bones of the inequalisation criterion which has been christened the employment-corrected double factorial terms of trade (ECDFTT).

Before leaping, however, from the abstractions of the previous chapter's model to real world data, some preliminary steps must be taken.

1. GROWING LABOUR FORCE

A constant labour force was assumed when theorising about the direction of the ECDFTT in Chapter V. To take on board the welfare implications of a growing labour force it was suggested in Chapter IV that the ECDFTT should be normalised:

$$\text{normalised ECDFTT} \equiv \frac{P\Pi_c N_c \div N}{\Pi_m^*} \equiv \frac{P_c \Pi_c N_c \div N}{P_m \Pi_m^*} \equiv \frac{V_c \div N}{P_m \Pi_m^*}, \qquad \text{(VI.1)}$$

where the notation is as in Chapter IV. This is obviously a generalisation of the un-normalised ECDFTT and reduces back to it when N is constant.

This generalisation recognises that an increase of employment due to the pressure of a growing labour force does not have the same welfare significance as an increase which reduces the initial stock of workers who were either formally unemployed or had a zero marginal product. Employment growth in Southland's C-producing sector contributes towards convergence of living standards in relation to Northland only insofar as the *share* of its total labour force employed in C-production itself grows.

There is, however, a less tractable problem if we are interested, as we obviously are, not in convergence or divergence *per se* but in that part which can be attributed to 'the system', to the inherited pattern of specialisation.

If in one country the labour force rises faster than in the other, this will be a factor pushing towards deterioration of the relative price of that country's exports via enhanced supply pressure. If as a result the ECDFTT moved against that country, this could not be blamed on the pattern of specialisation for the simple but sufficient reason that, in the context of the model used in the previous chapter, either country could bring an inequalising effect on itself if its labour force grew sufficiently faster than the other's.

This is a serious problem because the labour force in developing countries has grown faster than in developed countries and unless this is netted out any empirical findings will be subject to a question mark.

For the present purpose the growth of the labour force may be viewed as exogenous. In a special case the solution of the problem is then simple. Suppose we change from a (first) scenario in which the growth rate of Southland's labour force (and an associated proportionate growth of employment) is greater than Northland's, to a (second) scenario in which it is the same. And suppose that as employment in Southland grows more slowly under the second scenario, there is an offsetting rise (or smaller fall) in relative price, so that the growth of aggregate real income in Southland is the same under both scenarios. A price elasticity of demand for C lower than unity by an amount which depends on the proportion of total C-output produced in Southland will bring about this result. In the second scenario the growth rate of Southland's real income per head will be higher than in the first in proportion to the difference in the growth rates of the respective labour forces under the first scenario. The inequalisation generated by the second scenario could then be simulated from data of the first by normalising the ECDFTT by an index of Northland's labour force:

$$\text{normalised ECDFTT (second version)} \equiv \frac{P\Pi_c N_c \div N^*}{\Pi_m^*} \equiv \frac{V_c \div N^*}{P_m \Pi_m^*}. \qquad \text{(VI.2)}$$

This is obviously a special case but it may be no worse as an approximation than that which a full fledged application of counter-factual methodology, which is now widely viewed with cynicism, would yield.

What makes the special case especially interesting and much more acceptable is a coincidence which will be noted in the next section.

2. URBANISATION

Since the bulk of non-fuel primary production is agricultural, the growth of the relevant labour force is affected not only by population growth, age structure, and participation rates but by the phenomenon of urbanisation which has been very pronounced in the developing world.

In the model of the previous chapter there was no urban sector as such in Southland (though there was nothing to preclude the primitive sector from having an urban component). So urbanisation must be viewed as exogenous. It then follows that the relevant labour force for normalising the ECDFTT for agricultural commodities is the agricultural labour force.

This happens to have grown in developing countries as a group over the years in which we are interested at almost exactly the same rate as the total labour force in developed countries: with 1970 = 100, the respective index numbers were 92 and 89 in 1960; 109 and 109 in 1977 (Food and Agricultural Organisation (FAO) *Production Yearbook*). The coincidence is very convenient because it gives a validity to the developed countries' labour force as the normaliser, as in expression (VI.2), which it could not hope to have without it.

3. INDICES

In proceeding to construct indices of the ECDFTT a line will first be drawn between exhaustible commodities (minerals) and reproducible commodities (agricultural products). As explained at greater length in Chapter IV, section 5, the basic difference between them, in the present context, is that exhaustible commodities have a built-in upward price tendency[1] which may be viewed (in part) as compensation for the depletion of resources, hence the welfare-neutral position for a natural-resource exporter is represented not by a constant ECDFTT index but by a rising one—slowly perhaps, but rising nevertheless.

So in the first place normalised ECDFTT indices (in the two versions represented by expressions (VI.1) and (VI.2)) are calculated for the minerals of developing market economies (excluding fuels which are petroleum-dominated) *vis-à-vis* manufactures of developed market economies—see columns **13** and **14** of Table VI.1. As throughout this work, the classification into developed and developing market economies is that of the UN Secretariat unless otherwise stated.

The value index of the developing market economies' mineral output can only be proxied by the value index of their mineral exports.[2] This is not a bad proxy, given the high proportion of the developing countries' mineral output which is exported. But in order to limit reliance on a proxy, the subgroup of non-ferrous metals (which accounted for nearly half of the developing countries' non-fuel mineral exports in 1970) is considered separately. For this subgroup, the value of output in developing countries, in addition to being proxied by exports, is obtained by multiplying output volumes by US prices. Versions (VI.1) and (VI.2) of the ECDFTT index are calculated in both cases, giving four series for non-ferrous metals (columns **15–18**).

The ECDFTT indices for agricultural products as a whole are given in columns **27** and **28**. But again a value-of-output index is proxied by a value-of-exports index, and in this instance the proxy is much less good than in the case of minerals.

To reduce reliance on an untested proxy, six commodities were selected so that the value of their output, in addition to being proxied by exports, could be calculated as the product of volume of output and export unit value. The six were the only agricultural commodities which simultaneously satisfied a double criterion of importance: in 1970 each had a share of at least 1 per cent in total exports of developing market economies and such economies accounted for at least half of the total world exports of the commodities concerned. The selected sample comprised cocoa, coffee, cotton, natural rubber, sugar, and tea. Columns **19–22** give the four alternative series for the ECDFTT of these commodities.

A subset of four commodities—cocoa, coffee, natural rubber, and tea—was extracted for separate calculation and the four ECDFTT series concerning this subset are given in columns **23–26**. The reason for separating them relates to the condition which, in Chapter IV, section 3, was said to be needed for the unweighted DFTT and, by extension, the unweighted ECDFTT, to be an appropriate index of inequalisation—namely, that the import shares of the two groups of countries should sum to one ($\omega + \omega^* = 1$). The obverse of this in a model of complete specialisation is that the shares of exportables retained for home consumption should also sum to one. Since the developed market economies retain 90 per cent of their manufactured output, the commodities which may be properly paired with manufactures in these calculations are those of which the developing countries retain only a small fraction. *Grosso modo* this may be said to be

TABLE
Indices of employment-corrected double factorial

	Developing countries					
	Value of mineral exports except fuels	Value of exports of non-ferrous metals	Production of non-ferrous metals valued at US prices[1]	Value of exports of six crops[2]	Production of six crops valued at export unit values[2]	Value of exports of four crops[3]
SITC classes	27+28 +67+68	68		0721 +0711 +2631 +2311 +0611 +0612 +0741		0721 +0711 +2311 +0741
	1	2	3	4	5	6
Year 1960	40	38	43	79	77	84
1961	41	38	41	74	76	73
1962	41	40	41	70	73	73
1963	43	40	44	77	79	74
1964	52	47	50	81	85	81
1965	58	54	57	79	88	78
1966	66	68	58	80	80	79
1967	67	69	61	89	82	77
1968	74	81	72	82	82	83
1969	86	96	82	88	90	89
1970	100	100	100	100	100	100
1971	83	75	94	94	105	89
1972	97	77	101	105	113	96
1973	133	124	125	143	144	135
1974	213	191	182	193	253[6]	153
1975	187	119	157	194	255	145
1976	189	153	178	218	233	228
1977	198	160		276	322[6]	322
1978	214	165		276	317	318
Value in 1970 in $000000	7400	3540	5272	8926	14581	5542

VI.1
terms of trade and their component parts 1960–78

Developing countries			Developed countries		
Production of four crops valued at export unit values [3]	Value of all agricultural exports	Value of all primary exports except fuels	Economically active population[4]		Average product of labour in manufacturing valued at export unit values
	0+1+2+4 except 27 & 28	0+1+2+4 +67+68			
7	**8**	**9**	**10**	**11**	**12**
89	71	63	84	89	58
83	69	62	85	90	61
81	71	63	87	91	63
78	77	68	88	92	65
86	81	73	89	93	69
95	82	75	90	94	74
81	83	78	92	96	78
84	81	77	94	97	81
79	85	82	96	98	83
93	91	90	98	99	92
100	100	100	100	100	100
99	101	96	102	101	110
101	118	112	105	102	127
126	168	159	107	104	159
170	214	214	109	105	194
154	208	203	112	106	212
219	248	232	114	108	232
399[6]	303	275	117	109	259
368	319	291	120	110	305
6765	20070	27470			

[*see pp. 108–9 for Table VI.1 cont., and p. 110 for Sources and Notes*]

Table VI.1 (*cont.*)

	Developing countries' ECDFTT for various primary product groups					
	Minerals except fuels		Non-ferrous metals			
Procedure[5]	IA	IB	IA	IIA	IB	IIB
	13	14	15	16	17	18
	1 / 10 X 12	1 / 11 X 12	2 / 10 X 12	3 / 10 X 12	2 / 11 X 12	3 / 11 X 12
Year 1960	82	77	78	88	73	83
1961	79	75	73	79	69	75
1962	75	72	73	75	70	72
1963	75	72	70	77	67	73
1964	85	81	77	82	73	78
1965	87	83	81	85	77	81
1966	92	88	94	81	91	77
1967	88	85	91	80	87	77
1968	92	91	101	90	100	89
1969	96	95	107	91	105	90
1970	100	100	100	100	100	100
1971	74	75	67	84	68	85
1972	73	75	58	76	59	78
1973	78	81	73	74	75	76
1974	101	104	91	86	94	89
1975	79	83	50	66	53	70
1976	72	75	58	67	61	71
1977	65	70	53		57	
1978	58	64	45		49	
Implicit compound annual rate of change* 1960 to 1977	-0.0042	-0.0034	-0.167	-0.0064[7]	-0.0088	-0.0014[7]
	(-0.74)	(-0.63)	(-1.72)	(-1.23)	(-0.94)	(-0.28)
	[1.077]	[1.108]	[0.989]	[1.065]	[1.019]	[1.112]
1960 to 1974	-0.0067	0.014	0.0042	0.0025	0.0112	0.0096
	(-1.01)	(2.22)	(0.39)	(0.49)	(1.07)	(1.89)
	[1.191]	[1.250]	[0.812]	[1.156]	[0.858]	[1.204]

* *T*-ratio in parentheses; Durbin-Watson statistic in square brackets.

vis-à-vis developed countries' manufactures									
Six crops[2]				Four crops[3]				All agricultural products	
IA	IIA	IB	IIB	IA	IIA	IB	IIB	IA	IB
19	**20**	**21**	**22**	**23**	**24**	**25**	**26**	**27**	**28**
4	**5**	**4**	**5**	**6**	**7**	**6**	**7**	**8**	**8**
10 × 12	**10 × 12**	**11 × 12**	**11 × 12**	**10 × 12**	**10 × 12**	**11 × 12**	**11 × 12**	**10 × 12**	**11 × 12**
161	157	152	148	171	182	162	171	145	137
142	146	135	138	140	160	133	151	133	125
127	133	123	128	133	147	128	142	129	125
135	139	128	132	130	137	123	130	135	128
133	139	127	133	133	141	127	134	133	127
118	131	113	126	116	142	111	136	122	117
111	111	107	107	110	112	105	108	115	111
117	108	113	104	101	111	97	106	107	103
102	102	101	101	104	99	102	98	106	105
98	100	97	99	99	103	98	102	101	100
100	100	100	100	100	100	100	100	100	100
84	94	85	95	79	88	80	89	90	91
79	85	81	87	72	76	74	78	89	91
84	85	87	87	79	74	82	76	99	102
91	120[6]	95	124[6]	73	81	75	83	101	105
82	108	86	113	61	65	64	68	88	92
83	88	87	93	86	83	91	87	94	99
91	106[6]	98	114[6]	106	132[6]	114	141[6]	100	107
75	87	82	95	87	101	95	110	87	95
−0.0378	−0.0280	−0.0302	−0.0204	−0.0430	−0.0449	−0.0353	−0.0373	−0.0269	−0.0193
(−9.99)	(−5.05)	(−7.79)	(−3.58)	(−6.37)	(−5.47)	(−5.09)	(−4.45)	(−8.20)	(−5.63)
[1.071]	[1.106]	[0.976]	[1.044]	[0.961]	[0.899]	[0.927]	[0.867]	[0.863]	[0.823]
−0.0455	−0.0377	−0.0383	−0.0309	−0.0560	−0.0613	−0.0491	−0.0544	−0.0325	−0.0254
(−11.36)	(−5.86)	(−9.71)	(−4.75)	(−14.49)	(−15.73)	(−12.55)	(−14.50)	(−8.92)	(−6.75)
[1.633]	[1.221]	[1.504]	[1.183]	[1.903]	[1.840]	[1.930]	[1.793]	[0.904]	[0.875]

[*see p. 110 for Sources and Notes*]

the case for the four agricultural commodities (and for the metals), but not for cotton and sugar of which the share retained by developing countries exceeds two-thirds.[3]

For the totality of agricultural products (columns **27** and **28**) $\omega + \omega^* = 1$ is not satisfied, but this is immaterial because in their case, over the relevant period, the relative price component of their ECDFTT was free of statistically significant trend.[4]

An important line along which disaggregation is called for is that which divides commodities which are confronted by the production of close substitutes in developed countries from those which are not. The separation of the four commodities from the group of six can serve this purpose also. Of the four, only natural rubber faces a reasonably

---

Sources for Table VI.1

Column **1**: difference between columns **9** and **8**.

Column **2**: UNCTAD, *Handbook of International Trade and Development Statistics 1976* and UN, *Monthly Bulletin of Statistics* (various issues), special tables.

Column **3**: C. J. Schmitz, *World Non-Ferrous Metal Production and Prices 1700–1976* (London, Frank Cass, 1979).

Columns **4** & **6**: FAO data bank and FAO, *Trade Yearbook* (various issues).

Columns **5** & **7**: as for columns **4** and **6** plus FAO, *World Crop Statistics 1948–64* and FAO, *Production Yearbook* (various issues).

Columns **8** & **9**: as for column **2**.

Columns **10** & **11**: FAO, *Production Yearbook* (various issues).

Column **12**: For average product data—UN, *Statistical Yearbook 1978*, with data for non-reported years supplied directly by UN Secretariat. For export unit values—up to 1975, World Bank, *Price Prospects for Major Primary Commodities* (Report No. 814/77, June 1977); extended to 1977 with the aid of UN, *Statistical Yearbook 1977*.

Notes to Table VI.1

[1] The following metals are included: antimony, copper, lead, mercury, nickel, silver, tin, zinc.

[2] Cocoa, coffee, cotton, rubber, sugar, tea. In column **5** only centrifugal sugar is included.

[3] Cocoa, coffee, rubber, tea.

[4] Years 1961–4, 1966–9, and 1971–4 interpolated.

[5] In procedure I the value of the developing countries' production is proxied by the value of exports, while in II it is obtained by multiplying current output by current quoted prices or current export unit values. In procedure A the employment normalisation is with respect to the total economically active population in developing countries, while in B it is with respect to the same in developed countries.

[6] There is a freak element in these results when, in constructing indices under procedure II, large current-year crops are valued at high current export unit values which reflect low crops in the previous year.

[7] Relates to 1960–76.

close substitute in the shape of synthetic rubber, but not too close because of marked features specific to natural rubber. Cotton, on the other hand, has synthetic fibres to contend with and cane sugar is faced by the virtually perfect substitute of beet sugar produced in developed market economies.

The first twelve columns of Table VI.1 give the component series from which the ECDFTT indices set out in the remaining columns were calculated. A comment is called for only in the case of column **12**, which contains the index for the value of the average product of labour in manufacturing in developed market economies. This could be obtained in two ways: either by multiplying a physical productivity index by an export unit value index (the latter serving also as the price of all domestically produced manufactures[5]), or by dividing value added in manufacturing (aggregated across countries at current exchange rates) by the related numbers employed. The former was deliberately chosen because where the two differ—basically in the years 1972–4—it incorporates the more appropriate price structure.[6]

The statistic which summarises the direction and magnitude of the movement of the ECDFTT indices is given at the foot of columns **13** to **28** in the two rows labelled 'implicit annual rate of change'. The first row relates to the 1960-77 period as a whole and the second to the period 1960-74. The initial year (1960) is dictated by data availability. But the choice of 1977 as a terminal year for purposes of trend estimation is deliberate. (The tabulated series extend to 1978.) That year marked a pronounced peak in all ECDFTT series for agricultural products, regardless of the degree of aggregation. When the maintained hypothesis is that the ECDFTT will deteriorate, it will be more searchingly tested if the period chosen ends in a year most favourable to the negative.

The reason for looking separately at a shorter period, 1960-74, is that after 1974 unemployment set in in the developed market economies, whereas the ECDFTT index was established as a criterion of inequalisation on the explicit assumption of full employment in one of the trading partners (the developed countries). As it happens, no significant difference in the results obtained for the two sample periods emerges and the distinction, though important in principle, will be de-emphasised *de facto*. Note, however, that once again the period ends in a peak year for the ECDFTT.

The summary statistic of trend in the Table VI.1 is the value of r obtained from a semi-loglinear regression of the form

$$\ln(\text{ECDFTT}) = \text{constant} + rt$$

where t is time in years. One way of viewing this equation is as the super-reduced form of the model of Chapter V. This would be of course heroic econometric 'aggregation' but any attempt at estimation of individual coefficients of the model, if not open to scepticism on general grounds, is ruled out by paucity of data. The most modest but perhaps most becoming view is that we are interested in r as a summary of the record, not as the best estimate of a stable coefficient. What ultimately matters most is whether r is significantly different from zero and, if so, whether it is positive or negative.

At a glance it can be seen that in all cases but one where the result is statistically significant at the 5 per cent level, the ECDFTT indices deteriorate. Significant deterioration is concentrated in columns **19–28.**[7] The non-significant results (columns **13–18**) relate to minerals (with one marginal exception, or two, if a one-tail test is applied), which is entirely unsurprising. Recall that compensation for depletion of natural resources requires a rising ECDFTT to keep resource exporters on the equalisation/inequalisation borderline. The trendlessness of the data need not therefore imply an exception to the deteriorating position recorded with respect to the agricultural commodities in the remaining columns.

The six selected agricultural products (which in 1970 accounted for nearly 45 per cent of all agricultural exports of developing market economies) registered a substantial decline in all four versions of the ECDFTT index, ranging from 2.0 to 4.5 per cent per annum.

The rate of deterioration was markedly faster for the subgroup of four crops. This too is unsurprising, given that the two excluded crops are both less export-oriented and can displace closer substitutes in developed market economies (though in the case of sugar, substitution is thwarted by the very tight protection operated by many developed market economies).

For all agricultural products together, the recorded rate of deterioration ranges from about 2 per cent per annum to over 3 per cent. Caution is needed here because the value of output is proxied by exports and there is no independent measure of it. Unlike minerals, the share of exports in the total agricultural output of developing market economies is small even if we net out (as we should) the output of primitive agriculture. Two questions appear critical in interpreting the evidence of columns **27** and **28.** First, which is growing faster: output or exports? If the latter, as the model would suggest and as has been typically the case for tradeable goods in the period covered by the data, the true deterioration would be greater than recorded in Table VI.1. Second, does the growth of downstream processing in producing countries mean that there is an underestimation of the growth of agricultural exports (SITC classes 0, 1, 2, and 4 except 27 and 28) because raw cotton is now exported as a component of cotton fabrics, hides and skins as footwear, timber as plywood or furniture, etc.? The answer is not obvious because at the same time an increasing amount of manufacturing tends to be incorporated in products which continue to be entered in the same broad SITC classes as raw agricultural commodities, for example cocoa beans transformed, prior to export, into cocoa butter, loose tea into packet tea or tea in teabags. By looking roughly at data at the SITC three-digit level it is possible to place an upper bound of ±0.5 per cent per annum on the bias from growing downstream processing.

Thus, while it would be unwise to throw caution to the wind, the evidence of deterioration of the ECDFTT for the aggregate of agricultural products which columns **27** and **28** provide cannot be dismissed lightly.

As a number of agricultural products can in principle displace near-perfect substitutes produced in developed market economies, the persistence of deterioration must be accounted for by one or more of the following reasons: (a) products such as coffee and cocoa which cannot displace (because they do not compete against) close substitutes, dominate those which can; (b) displacement potential fails to be reflected in actual displacement because of growing protectionism by developed countries; (c) displacement is thwarted by a mechanism such as that incorporated in the model of the preceding sections, which triggers off increases in productivity in the primary sector of developed market economies as some workers are induced to transfer out of it by price movements adverse to the primary sector.

Viewing jointly the evidence for minerals and agricultural products the conclusion must be that the ECDFTT for the entire commodity-producing sector of developing countries were effectively deteriorating over the period of the data.

4. CAUTIONS

Some cautionary points applicable to all the calculations will now be added, together with certain considerations which place their significance in perspective.

In principle, the labour productivity components of the ECDFTT indices must be measured after deducting from output the capital input required to sustain the observed productivity growth rate. The material for such netting out is not available for developing market economies. But it should be noted that if the investment required to sustain the observed growth rate were a constant fraction of output, the net and gross productivity indices would behave indentically.

In the case of minerals netting out would have pushed their ECDFTT towards deterioration if, as is widely believed, the capital/output ratio in mineral extraction kept increasing in the sixties and seventies while, in contrast, the capital/output ratio in manufacturing in developed market economies was apparently steady.[8]

Netting out purchased inputs to obtain value added in primary production (instead of operating *de facto* with value of gross output) would also have been desirable. In the agricultural sector of developed market economies the ratio of purchased inputs to value added has grown dramatically. If the same has been true of developing economies, the computed deterioration of their agricultural ECDFTT in Table VI.1 would be an underestimate.

Likewise changes in work/leisure proportions should in principle be taken into account, with utility being assigned to leisure as well as consumption. Over the period of the data the average weekly hours worked in developed market economies appears to have fallen slightly. For wage employees in developing market economies they may have fallen even more, but for owner/cultivators who dominate most crops it is impossible to tell.

The period 1960–77 is too short to permit confident conclusions about long-term trends. But the most likely source of short-term bias can be ruled out: this was not a period of cyclical downswing in the relative price of primary products. It was, however, a period of historically untypical rapid productivity growth in developed market economies: growth of output per head has dominated the growth of output due to more heads. A reversal of this would be associated with income elasticities closer to unity for all goods (as the consumption pattern of extra heads would tend to replicate that of existing heads), in which event a critical influence pushing towards deteriorating ECDFTT would push less vigorously. (In terms of the model of Chapter V, a slowing down of productivity growth in developed countries will typically lower the rate of growth of absolute income per head in developing countries. The latter has not been a concern of this monograph but it is worth noting that slower relative deterioration in developing countries could be associated with slower absolute improvement.)

The period covered by the data, in addition to being short, has two distinct phases—at least for the agricultural products: a sharp ECDFTT deterioration in the years 1960–71 followed by near-trendlessness in the subsequent years included in Table VI.1. Since some cyclicity of movement is to be expected, it may be viewed as an advantage that the sample period does not contain just a phase of monotonic movement. Of course, it could be argued that the post-1971 phase is the swallow which marks the beginning of a permanent spring for the developing countries' primary sector activities. But against such an optimistic interpretation stands the fact that by stopping in 1978 (owing to incompleteness of data for subsequent years at the time of writing) Table VI.1 fails to convey the untypical nature of the years 1974-7, a period dominated by the huge but ephemeral rise in the price of coffee in 1977 owing to heavy frosts in Brazil and a period marked also by a temporary upsurge of restrictive supply management for a number of commodities, and by the once-over price-enhancing effect of cartelisation of petroleum in 1973 on such commodities as natural rubber and cotton (via the higher costs inflicted on their petroleum-based synthetic substitutes) and on sugar (via increased demand for energy-producing substitutes for oil).

Recall, anyway, that in order to make the hypothesis of ECDFTT deterioration jump through the most optimistic hoops, the data set was truncated at the local peak of 1977 for purposes of trend estimation.

Non-resident ownership of enterprises in developing countries may create problems. One problem would arise if the non-resident share of value added showed a secular trend. But it needs to be a trend, not a once-over change, unless the once-over change is so big that it overshadows a prolonged trend in the observed ECDFTT. Another problem relates to transfer-pricing practices: prices received by producing countries may not move proportionately with prices recorded in terminal commodity markets. (This could also arise on account of long-term supply contracts, bilateral agreements or disproportionate changes in transport costs.) But except for non-ferrous metals, the series of Table VI.1 are based on export unit values, not market prices. In any case, export unit value indices and market price indices, though sometimes drifting apart in the short run, have not been diverging significantly over the entire period since 1960 (compare columns (4) and (5) of Table III.3).

The role of productivity growth calls for comment. The model of Chapter V would not give much mileage to the argument that commodity-producing countries should blame their slow productivity growth for the observed ECDFTT deterioration instead of their inherited pattern of specialisation. For commodities of agricultural origin there is no knowing how fast or slow productivity growth has been, but were it to become faster, producing countries would gain less on this score than they would lose from the associated fall in relative price in respect of the significant proportion of their exportables which they dominate as producers but absorb very lightly as consumers. Price-inelastic demand yields this result.

At least a couple of cautionary points arise from the presence in the real world of more sectors than were allowed for in the model of Chapter V and, in particular, of a manufacturing sector in the commodity-producing countries. First, an infant manufacturing sector has often been associated with import-substitution policies which, in the neoclassical view of the world, are in some sense anti-trade and in the same sense exert indirectly a restrictive influence on exportables-producing sectors. Second, given balanced trade, the rapid expansion of exports of manufactures from developing market economies which has taken place must, arguably, have as a counterpart a restricting influence on primary exportables. If either of these points lay at the back of the observed deterioration of the ECDFTT, the deterioration could not be blamed on the traditional pattern of specialisation.

A priori these points are worthy of attention. Regarding the empirical plausibility of the first, it is generally agreed that by the 1970s the intensity of import-substituting policies had passed its peak. Even if not waning, such policies would affect adversely the ECDFTT only via their restrictive influence on goods facing close substitutes in developed market economies and this would be compensated by goods facing weak substitutes with respect to which a restrictive influence would benefit the ECDFTT, given the price-inelastic demand for such goods.

Regarding the second point, as the expansion of exports of manufactures has been heavily concentrated in a handful of developing countries, the remainder could not have been subject to the elbowing out of their primary exportables. Additionally, the sharp rise in the price of petroleum in 1973 has placed the non-oil producing countries under a much greater pressure to expand their primary exportables than any easing of such pressure that they may have experienced as a result of growing exports of manufactures.

Empirically, the presence of sectors additional to those which are directly influenced by the traditional pattern of specialisation is a bonus. This is because we can test whether they too contributed to inequalisation. If they did, the emphasis on the traditional pattern of international specialisation as a source of drag on developing economies is liable to be exaggerated, if not entirely misplaced. But apparently they did not. Table VI.2 shows that, with respect to all sectors combined, output per member of the labour force grew faster in developing than in developed market economies.[9] This is, of course, subject to the reservation that the statistics are very fragile and they do include oil-rich developing countries which in principle ought to be excluded (given that fuels have not been included in the primary products treated in this monograph).

Overshadowing every other consideration is the degree to which reality approximates the condition which validates the assumption that output growth in developing countries' exportables carries the same weight when associated with both productivity increases and employment increases (employment increases being understood as increases in the share of employment). The validating condition, it will be recalled, is that increased employment in exportables is not associated with any foregone employment elsewhere. This is plausible in the context of the prevailing heavy unemployment but is, nevertheless, a limit situation. If the share of employment in primary exportables increased but at the cost of some foregoing of other employment, the observed decline in the ECDFTT indexes would underestimate the deterioration of the developing countries' relative position attributable to trade-related sectors. The reverse would be the case if the share of employment in primary exportables decreased.

This brings us back to the question of employment in agricultural exportables in developing countries. Very fragmentary evidence suggests that the employment share of some crops in some of the older producing countries has undergone some contraction. But, unsurprisingly,

TABLE VI.2

Growth of GDP at 1975 prices per unit of the labour force

	Developing countries[1]	Industrialised countries
1960–70	4.1	3.7
1970–7	3.3[2]	2.6[3]

Source: World Bank, *World Development Report 1979* (August 1979).

Notes to Table VI.2

[1] The World Bank's category 'developing countries' and the UN's 'developing market economies' are not identical: the differences relate mainly to Cuba, Greece, Israel, Portugal, South Africa, Spain, and Yugoslavia.

[2] The annual rate of growth of GDP in 1970–7 minus annual growth rate of labour force in 1970–80.

[3] Annual rate of growth of GDP in 1970–8 minus annual growth rate of labour force in 1970–7.

newer producers have experienced large expansion. The balance cannot be determined on the evidence. But, for what it is worth, the model of Chapter V implies an overall expansion. (See also Chapter VII, section 3.)

5. CONCLUSION

The evidence assembled here is consistent with the view that the traditional exchange of primary exports against imports of manufactures has been conducive to making growth incrementally inequalising for developing market economies.

The index which has been employed to test inequalisation has three dimensions—relative price, productivity, and employment—and is therefore more comprehensive than anything which has been used before.

But clearly not all the finer points are captured, nor are the data which have been used fully satisfactory in either quality or length of coverage. It is an open question whether, had it been possible to resort to econometric modelling and estimation, the results would have been subject to fewer reservations—probably not, given the numerous degress of discretion in model specification, lag structures, choice of proxies, etc. In any event there are grounds for caution and there is great scope for further research.

VII

STALLED SEARCH FOR TWO-DIMENSIONAL INDICES

The development of the employment-corrected doubled factorial terms of trade (ECDFTT) index as a criterion of incremental inequalisation served two purposes simultaneously: it allowed for the employment dimension, which is important in the context of chronic unemployment in developing countries, and it circumvented the need for estimates of productivity growth in the traditional exportables of developing countries without which the straight DFTT cannot be calculated.

The DFTT index omits, of course, the employment dimension but despite this it would have its uses. It would be appreciated by those who are happy to apply neoclassically-inspired full employment models to developing countries with equal marginal value products in all sectors. For the rest of us it would throw light on how the burden of the observed inequalisation is apportioned between employment and productivity. And it would help those who, like Lewis (1969), assign a central role to the DFTT in their models or those who, like Amin (1976), hope to use a DFTT index to test their theories.

To calculate an index for the DFTT it is necessary to have employment data. In conjunction with output data, they will yield average productivity estimates which can be plugged directly into the DFTT formula or, in conjunction with ECDFTT indices, they can lead to the DFTT destination by another route since, by definition,

$$\text{DFTT} \equiv P\frac{\Pi_c}{\Pi_m^*} \equiv \frac{P_c\Pi_c}{P_m\Pi_m^*} \equiv \frac{V_c \div N_c}{P_m\Pi_m^*} \equiv \text{ECDFTT} \div N_c,$$

where the notation is the same as in Chapter IV.

The DFTT for metals can be easily, if roughly, computed from existing data and this is done in section 2.

1. A METHOD FOR ESTIMATING CHANGES OF EMPLOYMENT IN THE ABSENCE OF DIRECT DATA

There is, however, a daunting data barrier with regard to the labour force engaged in agricultural exportables, which hundreds of man-days of effort have failed to crack. Agricultural and population censuses either do not contain relevant data or the data are non-comparable over time. Sample surveys are numerous but overwhelmingly one-off affairs, which cannot therefore provide time series data. Areas under a crop are regularly reported but turn out to be a poor proxy for labour.

High hopes were entertained for the formula $(N_1 L_1^i / L_1)/(N_0 L_0^i / L_0)$ as a proxy for the index of the labour force in the *i*th crop (N_1^i / N_0^i), where N is the economically active population in all agriculture, N^i the labour force engaged in the *i*th crop, L the total cultivated area and L^i the area devoted to the *i*th crop; the subscripts $_0$ and $_1$ refer to the initial and terminal periods, respectively.

For all the variables in the formula statistics are available in publications of the UN and its agencies for at least some key years since 1960, extending over many developing countries and covering many crops. Some of the statistics are so obviously inconsistent that they have to be discarded, but with the rest it is in principle possible to compute indices for N^i by country. These would be perfect proxies for employment in the crops concerned if in each country the labour/land ratio in the *i*th crop changed in the same proportion as the labour/land ratio in the country's total agricultural sector, i.e. if

$$\frac{N_1^i / L_1^i}{N_0^i / L_0^i} = \frac{N_1 / L_1}{N_0 / L_0}.$$

If deviations from this occurred but were unbiased, they would still cancel out when aggregating for a crop across many countries.

However, without being tested, the formula cannot command confidence. Direct employment data by crop in some individual countries would have helped in testing it but prolonged searches for such data gave a meagre result. So in the end the formula was deemed too speculative to pursue here.

The paucity of direct data arises in part from severe practical difficulties in measuring employment in a crop.

The farmer who divides his labour between a commercial crop and the cultivation of a small plot for his family's food requirements must in principle have his time allocated between the two. The same holds for the person who busies himself with a commerical crop during seasonal peaks but migrates to a nearby town to act as a casual labourer for the rest of the time, or the person who participates in seasonal migrations between areas which grow crops with different seasonal peaks.

Analogous problems are not unknown in the North but they are so much more acute in the South that, following Myrdal (1968, Vol. II, pp. 1019-28), some writers are led to treat conventional concepts of employment/unemployment as inapplicable in developing countries.

In the circumstances only brief and broad observations on the DFTT of the developing countries' agricultural exportables will be ventured in section 3. In the meantime section 2 will look at the DFTT for metals.

2. THE DFTT BETWEEN METALS AND MANUFACTURES

The UN Secretariat compiles indices of labour productivity by industrial sector for developed and developing market economies respectively. The index for the manufacturing sector (ISIC class 3) of developed market economies can stand for Π_m^* and is set out in column (4) of Table VII.1. For Π_c two three-digit sectors in developing countries need to be combined: metal ore mining (ISIC class 230) and basic metal industries (ISIC class 37). The respective sectoral indices are set out in columns (1) and (2) and they are combined by unweighted averaging in column (3). ('Unweighted', because the sectoral weights are roughly equal in the base year 1970 regardless of whether production or employment weights are used.)[1] The resulting series for Π_c is least inconsistent with the series for P which is set out in column (6).[2]

Column (7) of Table VII.1 displays the DFTT series obtained by combining the parts set out in previous columns. As in Chapter VI, the implicit rate of change per unit time is obtained by semi-logarithmic regression on time over two periods, 1960-77 and 1960-74. (The reasons for the truncation in 1974 is the same as in Chapter VI.) For both periods the rate of change has a negative sign, indicating a declining trend in the DFTT of the developing countries for metals. But for the period 1960-74 the T-ratio signals that the calculated rate of change is not significantly different from zero at the 5 per cent level,

TABLE VII.1

Labour productivity, net barter terms of trade and double factorial terms of trade: metals of developing countries/manufactures of developed countries, 1960–77

1970 = 100

Year	Labour productivity						
	Developing countries						
	Metal ore mining[1] (1)	Basic metal industries[2] (2)	Average [(1) + (2)] ÷ 2 (3)	Developed countries' manufactures[3] (4)	Productivity ratio (3) ÷ (4) (5)	NBTT[4] (6)	DFTT (5) × (6) (7)
1960	77	82	79	68	116	72	84
1961	78	82	80	71	113	72	81
1962	80	83	81	74	109	74	81
1963	82	85	83	76	109	73	80
1964	85	85	85	80	106	80	85
1965	88	87	87	84	104	91	95
1966	89	91	90	87	103	101	104
1967	94	96	95	89	107	96	103
1968	99	101	100	92	109	97	106
1969	106	105	105	98	107	102	109
1970	100	100	100	100	100	100	100
1971	100	93	96	104	92	84	77
1972	104	95	99	110	90	75	67
1973	105	79	92	116	79	87	69

1974	104	80	92	116	79	97	77
1975	96	80	88	112	79	73	58
1976	99	87	93	122	76	73	55
1977	103	88	95	125	76	68	59
Implicit compound annual rate of change (*T*-ratio in single brackets, Durbin–Watson statistic in double brackets).				1960–77			−0.0232 (−2.82) ((0.41))
				1960–74			−0.0068 (−0.70) ((0.40))

Sources

Columns (1), (2), and (4): UN, *Statistical Yearbook 1978*, with data for non-reported years supplied directly by UN Secretariat.
Column (6): World Bank, *Price Prospects for Major Primary Commodities* (Report No. 814/77, June 1977) for years up to 1975; extended to 1977 with the aid of UN, *Statistical Yearbook 1978*.

Notes to Table VII.1

[1] ISIC class 230.

[2] ISIC class 37.

[3] ISIC class 3.

[4] Index of export unit values for metals, minerals and ores, weighted by the export values of developing countries in 1970, divided by the unit value index of manufactured exports of developed countries (SITC classes 5–8 inclusive) also with 1970 weights. The commodities included in the numerator are: copper, lead, tin, zinc, bauxite, iron ore, manganese ore, and phosphate rock. Phosphate rock, while included in the price index (but with a weight of less than 4 per cent), is excluded from the productivity indices for ISIC classes 230 and 37. The remaining commodities in the price index accounted for roughly 90 per cent of the 1970 exports of developing countries originating in sectors which are included in the productivity indexes of columns (1) and (2). The World Bank's definition of developing countries does not exactly coincide with that of the UN Secretariat.

while for the period 1960-77 the significance which the *T*-ratio registers is exaggerated by pronounced serial correlation (see Durbin-Watson statistic at foot of column (7)) and must be deemed at best marginal, even before making allowance for the susceptibility of the metal price component of the DFTT to the cyclical downturn of industrial activity in the years 1975-7.

On this evidence, a hypothesis of deterioration of the DFTT for metals, if sustainable, must be formulated with caution and must rest part of the burden on considerations beyond the record of the DFTT index as computed here. Two considerations which were relevant to the ECDFTT for metals in the previous chapter are relevant again here.

The first relates to the fact/belief that in the relevant period the capital/output ratio in the developing countries' mining sector has undergone a marked increase, while the evidence (cited in the previous chapter) points against any corresponding increase of the capital/output ratio in the manufacturing sector of developed market economies. The implication of this is that a net DFTT index (net of the output per person needed for investment to reach the attained labour productivity growth) would have shown a more unfavourable trend than that of the gross index of column (7).

The second consideration relates to the depletion of natural resources. Since this is equivalent to capital consumption, which is not compensated for under a constant DFTT, a distributionally neutral position requires a rising DFTT for the natural resource exporters, of which there is certainly no evidence.

3. ON THE DFTT BETWEEN AGRICULTURAL PRODUCTS AND MANUFACTURES

As previously noted,

$$\text{DFTT} \equiv \text{ECDFTT} \div N_c.$$

So the DFTT will move less favourably or more adversely than the ECDFTT if N_c is rising. Translated to a growing labour force context (with the ECDFTT normalised accordingly), the DFTT will move less favourably or more adversely if N_c is rising faster than the total labour force.

Such an outcome is typical in the model of Chapter V. As productivity increases in the exportables-producing sector of developing countries, it raises living standards in that sector and this attracts labour from the primitive sector. In the model the situation will be otherwise only if adverse price movements more than offset the growth of productivity in exportables, in other words, if there is absolute immiserization, not just inequalisation. But this can be empirically excluded: though the South has had pockets of absolute immiserization since World War II, for the developing countries as a whole absolute living standards have risen in the sectors producing traditional exportables (alongside the whole of their economies) even when petroleum is excluded.

From this one would conclude that since the ECDFTT for agricultural exportables were found in the previous chapter to have deteriorated, the DFTT would have deteriorated also, only more so.

But in the absence of hard evidence there are grounds for caution—in particular, caution with respect to some of the major crops selected for separate attention in Chapter VI.

Restrictive supply management was excluded from the model of Chapter V yet coffee, which dominates the subset of four crops, was subjected in the sixties and seventies to active supply management by Brazil, sometimes acting alone, sometimes in conjunction with other coffee producers and sometimes within the framework of the International Coffee Agreement. Almost inevitably, restriction of supply falls on employment (and acreage), not productivity growth, since those who stay in coffee-growing continue to be impelled by competition to keep improving productivity. Indeed the large uprooting programme in Brazil—in the sixties the acreage was nearly halved—was itself instrumental in raising productivity by having its greatest impact on the lowest-yielding trees.

Nor did the model allow for trade unions or government-determined minimum wages which, by steadily pushing up wage costs, narrow the scope for employment increases. Yet these factors were present in the case of crops in which large and medium-sized estates play a substantial part.

Since these influences generally operated in commodities with price-inelastic demand, they raised price by more than they restricted output so that, but for them, the ECDFTT deterioration recorded in the previous chapter would have been even greater. But at the same time they increased the share of the observed deterioration borne by the employment component of the ECDFTT, while reducing that borne by productivity.

In the light of these considerations it would be rash to conclude confidently that the DFTT of the South's agricultural exportables should have recorded a significantly larger deterioration than the ECDFTT. But if they did not, certain anti-competitive practices can take the credit for it.

4. SUMMARY

The DFTT index for the developing economies' metals *vis-à-vis* the developed economies' manufactures does not register a very perceptible trend, but trendlessness fails to compensate for the resource depletion suffered by metal-exporting countries.

No empirical evidence can be adduced for the DFTT of the developing economies' agricultural exportables. The model of Chapter V implies that if (as reported in Chapter VI) the ECDFTT deteriorate, the DFTT must deteriorate faster. But this should be interpreted with caution because the model omits certain restrictive practices which would be expected to push the DFTT in the other direction.

VIII

POLICY TO STEM INEQUALISATION

If, as may be concluded from the preceding pages, the pattern of trade and specialisation which the developing countries have inherited from the colonial period is incrementally inequalising, what should they do about it?

This is obviously a vast question to which only a detailed and sharply focused examination can do full justice. But for the present purpose a broad brushwork approach will have to suffice.

The main thrust of the succeeding pages is captured by the twin headings: (1) price enhancement and (2) diversification. Both have been on the agenda for so long that where they do not generate ideological heat they beget boredom. But the findings of this monograph point unmistakably in their direction, and while some of the discussion which follows treads well-worn ground, it is always flavoured by the policy-related insights which spring from this work.

1. PRICE ENHANCEMENT

As background to the policy discussion it should perhaps be said that the incrementally inequalising effects of traditional specialisation would not call for policy action if market pressures were shifting the resources and causing a more appropriate pattern to be efficiently created.

But the market mechanism is fundamentally flawed, at least with respect to those commodities (tropical beverages, some major non-ferrous metals etc., accounting in total for over a quarter of the South's non-fuel primary exports to the North) which are subject to globally low price and income elasticities of demand, and are dominated by developing country producers who export the bulk of their output.

In the case of these commodities competing individual producers find it beneficial, indeed essential, to their survival, to contrive to avail themselves of opportunities to raise productivity. Collectively, however, they lose from adverse effects on prices so that, as the evidence implies, the realised productivity growth exceeds that which would have kept the developing countries on the equalisation/inequalisation borderline.

Additionally, for some commodities of great importance to many developing countries but in the world output of which the North has a substantial share (e.g. sugar), developing countries are faced by automatically adjusting barriers (such as the variable import levies of the European Economic Community) or barriers subject to discretionary (and not infrequent) adjustment, as a result of which there is exactly the same conflict between the individual and collective interests of developing country producers as described in the previous paragraph.

To limit output growth to the rate which would stem incremental inequalisation via successive price enhancements, producers need to act collectively because it does not pay them to do it individually.

The novel element in this statement is that collective price enhancement is needed to forestall continuing inequalisation, which is rather different from viewing it as a method for predatory exploitation of consumers.

(a) *Negligible deadweight burdens*

Price enhancement policies are often said (*inter alia* by Johnson (1977)) to be allocatively inefficient; they involve a deadweight burden and are not therefore a good way of bringing about a resource transfer across the North/South boundary.

It is, however, inexcusable that this argument has attained respectability. For it is a matter of elementary theory that, if price enhancement is to provide reliable gains for producers, demand must be strongly price-inelastic and, if it is so, the deadweight burden is small relatively to the redistributive transfer.

At the risk of insulting the theoretical competence of many readers, this can be shown in terms of Marshallian surplus as follows. In Figure VIII.1 a restriction of output from C_0 to C_1 raises the market-clearing price from P_{c0} to P_{c1}. The redistribution of surplus from consumers to producers is measured by the rectangle $P_{c0}AE_1P_{c1}$ while the deadweight loss is measured by the area E_0E_1B. The latter would vanish in the limit of zero-elastic demand.

To this may be added the observation that, if other prices contain a monopoly component, as the prices of the North's manufactures undoubtedly do, the deadweight burden of a price enhancement policy may even turn negative.

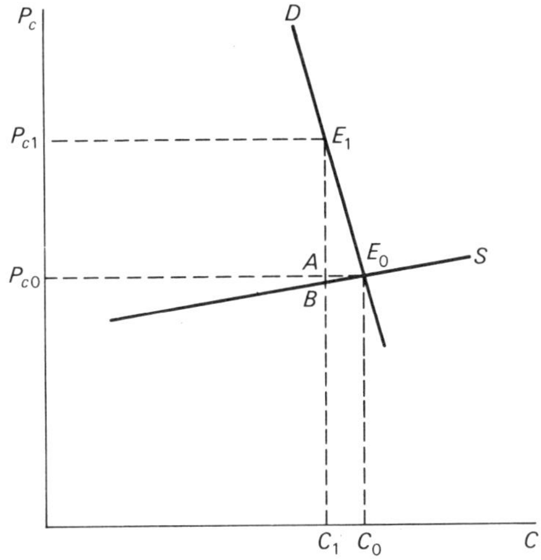

Figure VIII.1

(b) *Bilateral enhancement*

Developing countries have occasionally attempted to bring about price enhancement unilaterally by cartelising but, except in the case of petroleum, they have not persevered for long. They have, instead, pressed for bilaterally sponsored price enhancement by both producing and consuming countries. This indeed was one of the two major targets in the field of commodities—the other was price stabilisation—of the New International Economic Order which was launched by the Sixth Special Session of the General Assembly of the UN and entrusted to UNCTAD for its implementation.

The resolutions of the UN and its agencies are replete with references to 'remunerative' or 'just' or 'equitable' prices (for a selection of relevant quotations see Laszlo *et al.* (1978, pp. 45-65)), all of which mean to convey the idea of prices higher than those that the market left to itself would establish on average over good and bad years. But, in the event, the target of price enhancement has been smothered by overt and covert opposition from most developed countries, so that price enhancement has been pushed to the margin of international agendas despite the fact that the economics of price raising are technically much less demanding than the economics of price stabilising.

Even from the narrowest standpoint of their own immediate material welfare, is the opposition of developed countries to all price-enhancing action wise?

In analysing this issue it is useful to think in terms of two benchmarks. One benchmark is the competitive price; the other is the monopoly price attainable by unilateral cartelisation of producers.

The market price for the major primary commodities of developing countries does not quite coincide with the competitive price: there have been attempts at supply management by some producing countries with respect to some products; some international commodity agreements contain export quota provisions which are occasionally triggered off; big corporations exert oligopolistic/oligopsonistic power on some commodities. But the deviations from the competitive price are not very marked (nowhere near as marked as in the case of prices of manufactures), and the competitive price suits the developed countries which are substantial net importers of such commodities.

Compared with this benchmark the developed countries have much to lose by price enhancement: they would lose what the developing countries gained if the game was zero sum; they would lose more than the developing countries gained if it was a negative-sum game due to the alleged allocative inefficiency of price-raising schemes; and they would lose yet more if the price shock caused them difficulties of adjustment as was the case with the oil price shocks.

Thus it is not surprising that, viewing price enhancement against this benchmark, developed countries find it incompatible with their (short-term?) interests and are not prepared to participate in its bilateral implementation.

But it is not an immutable law of nature that the competitive price should be *the* benchmark. Everything depends on an assessment of what is the most plausible alternative to bilateral price enhancement. If it appeared that the developing countries were in the process of creating the cohesion and the momentum that would make unilateral price enhancement a realistic possibility, the monopoly price benchmark will loom large in the calculations of the developed countries. Bilateral enhancement would then come to be perceived as an option to be sought, just as, if time were to run backwards to 1973, the North would be offering to participate in a jointly operated price-raising scheme for petroleum.

The North's present view that the risk of unilateral extension of price enhancement beyond petroleum is small is based on a number of reasons of which two are the most basic: (i) the developing countries are believed to lack the cohesion to operate cartels; (ii) the technical conditions for a cartel to be profitably feasible are thought to be lacking.

Casual observation suggests that the first reason is valid at the present time. The second reason rests on a number of studies which conclude that for commodities other than petroleum, price enhancement would fail to provide long-run gains for producers because the loss of market share to non-cartel sources of supply would more than offset the price enhancement generated. (For one of the most judicious of such studies see Radetzki (1976).) This rests on faulty or, at any rate, incomplete analysis.

(c) *Simple theoretical treatment of a cartel which practices self-defence*

At the risk of causing some indigestion, a more rounded but still simple theoretical treatment will be attempted here because a false sense of security in the North is a poor background for policy making.

The conditions which, it is contended, are sufficient for profitable unilateral price enhancement are as follows:

(α) price-inelastic global demand for commodity;
(β) a high proportion of intiial output under the control of collaborating producers (cartel participants);
(γ) cohesion among cartel participants;
(δ) non-negligible set-up costs for potential new capacity;
(ϵ) no concerted retaliation by consumers.

The surprise, if any, in this list is that two further conditions have been omitted, namely

(ζ) low elasticity of supply from sources outside the cartel;
(η) low potential for the development of new substitutes for the cartelised commodity.

The faith in point (ii) of the preceding section is nurtured by the belief that conditions (ζ) and (η) are not satisfied, and this belief sustains the view that in the long run the loss of volume to be suffered by the cartelised producers will be larger than their gain from higher prices.

But failure of (ζ) and (η) in the long run is not enough. If alternative supply sources can materialise, but only after a substantial time lag, a cartel which exploits the lag can make large gains. Pindyck (1978)

calculates that this is so in the case of bauxite. Moreover, since the profit-maximising price path for a cartel subject to the threat of new entrants would involve in the initial stages higher prices than in the absence of such a threat (at least for exhaustible resources), it is not necessarily true, as Gilbert and Goldman (1978) show, that the dead-weight burden of a profit-maximising cartel is higher when it is not subject to the risk of new entrants than when it is.

More decisive, however, is the fact that a cartel cohesive enough to support an active policy for the defence of its territory will not allow the technical conditions of (ζ) and (η) to come into play at all. By keeping some capacity in mothballs and/or holding the required volume of stocks (in the case of storable commodities), and openly standing ready to use them in order to bring back at short notice the ruling price to a level that would make new capacity (whether of the same commodity or of substitutes) incapable of recouping its setting-up costs, the cartel would retain a high share of the market regardless of conditions (ζ) and (η).

That a strategy of incipient pre-emption, as this may be called, would render (ζ) and (η) redundant can be formally shown by a simple extension of the textbook theory of the firm. This extension bears an affinity with a group of oligopoly models (Pyatt 1971; Wenders 1971–2; Caves and Porter 1977; Spence 1977, 1979; Dixit 1979; Eaton and Lipsey 1979) which allow for the use of idle capacity as an instrument of entry deterrence.

In Figure VIII.2 MC_k is the marginal cost curve of producers who are prepared to cartelise while MC_r is that of the rival producers. The global demand curve is D while $D_k \equiv D - MC_r$. MR_k is the marginal revenue curve implicit in D_k.

The competitive (pre-cartel) price is P_{co} with total output at $Q_0 = Q_{k0}$ (the output of producers who are cartelisable) + Q_{r0} (the output of their future rivals).

If a cartel is formed which curtails supply (by curtailing highest cost production among its members) but passively accepts erosion of its market by rivals, the cartel price will be P_{cm}, associated with a total output Q_m, of which Q_{km} will be supplied by cartel members (because the cartel's profit-maximising condition $MC_k = MR_k$ is satisfied at this price/output combination) and Q_{rm} will be supplied by rivals (because as price takers their profit-maximising condition is $MC_r = P_{cm}$). The extent of the cartel-generated price enhancement (i.e. $(P_{cm}/P_{co}) - 1$) is in this case critically dependent on the slope of

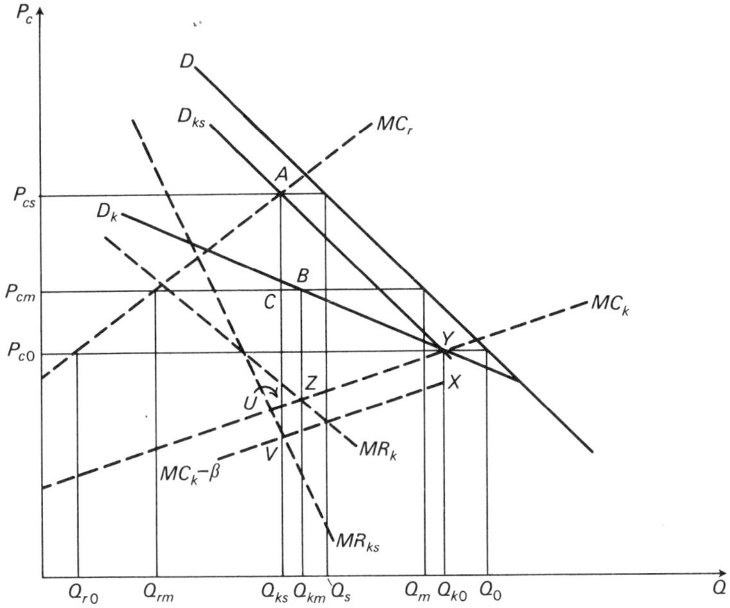

Figure VIII.2

the D_k curve. This in turn depends on the slope of the MC_r curve which, under the assumption of price-taking rivals, is the rival's supply curve. This, then, is the case in which condition (ζ) (and by extension condition (η)) has to be satisfied for cartel feasibility.

But a cartel which operates a strategy of incipient pre-emption will tolerate (because, for instance, it would be costly to dislodge) rival production equal to the pre-cartel volume Q_{r0} but no more. To prevent an increase in rival production the cartel will have to incur such cost as may be needed to make fully credible the threat that if necessary it will push prices back to a level which will render unprofitable any new capacity. While modelling the details of such a strategy is clearly difficult, one way of approaching it is to hypothesise that credibility depends on the cartel being able to raise market supplies to Q_0 at short notice. The cost of being able to do this may be viewed as proportional to the shortfall from the pre-cartel output, i.e. $\beta(Q_0 - Q)$ for $Q < Q_0$. The cost of the strategy is less the closer the post-cartel output is to Q_0, so that the marginal cost of the strategy is negative and $= -\beta$.

The marginal cost curve for the cartel (including the cost of pre-emption is then the dotted line labelled $MC_k - \beta$ in Figure VIII.2.

It can now be seen that under a self-defending cartel the price will be P_{cs}, at which price the cartel will sell Q_{ks}. This is determined by the first-order profit-maximising condition $MR_{ks} = MC_k - \beta$, where MR_{ks} is the marginal revenue curve implicit in $D_{ks} = D - Q_{ro}$.

Clearly, the height of P_{cs} is now wholly independent of the rival's supply curve (MC_r). Condition (ζ) is redundant and so, by extension, is (η).

But the following condition must be satisfied: the total cost of the pre-emption strategy (= area *UVXY*) must not equal or exceed the additional profit attributable to the strategy (= area $P_{cs}ACP_{cm}$ − area *BCUZ*).[1] To encompass this we should in principle add to conditions (α) to (ϵ) another one which, loosely phrased, would read:

(θ) low cost of deterrence strategy against outsiders.

The cost of mothballing capacity, to which monitoring the activities of rivals has to be added, is usually thought to be low.

If deterrence by threat fails (which it can do only if the credibility of the threat is inadequately established) actual price will have to be lowered for a time, which will affect the magnitude but not the sign of the long-run gain.

A sufficiently cohesive cartel can wield a carrot as well as a stick. It can make it attractive to developed country producers to participate in the cartel rather than erode its market share from the outside. The bauxite cartel, of which Australian producers are leading members, is a case in point.

With cohesion extending across commodities, the difficulty perceived as emanating from long-run expansion of substitutes can be obviated further: a cartel-induced rise in the price of, say, coffee will not encounter erosion of sales from consumers switching to tea or cocoa if all three are cartelised; ditto for aluminium, copper, lead, and tin.

(d) *North's dependence on non-cohesion of the South*

All this amounts to a dethronement of conditions (ζ) and (η), which have hitherto served to underpin scepticism about the feasibility of unilateral price enhancement for the South's major non-fuel commodities.

Of such commodities, the tropical beverages, some non-ferrous metals and a few others satisfy conditions (α), (β), and (γ). This leaves conditions (δ) and (ϵ)—cohesion of developing countries and retaliation by developed countries—as serious issues.

It has already been remarked that the cohesion condition is not satisfied, and the point will be taken up again promptly. With respect to retaliation, it may be observed that oil-importing developed countries got nowhere against OPEC. But in principle they can retaliate against unilateral price enhancement and by so doing claw back, at a cost, some of the cartel's gains. However, as compared with last-ditch defence by retaliation there will always be a bilaterally sponsored price enhancement up to a certain point which, by averting unilateral cartelisation, will involve a lower cost to the commodity-importing developed countries.

The point of all this is to make it clear that the opposition of developed countries to price-enhancing international commodity agreements can be said to be in their own material self-interest only because developing countries do not at present have the cohesion to bring about substantial unilateral price enhancement. But this is an unstable foundation for a policy for in effect it challenges the primary-producing countries to generate cohesion. If other circumstances conspire to create a favourable climate, as they did for OPEC in 1973, they may take up the challenge, in which event it may be too late for the countries of the North to become converted to bilateral price enhancement.

If before it is too late it were to be bilaterally agreed that the price enhancement component of international commodity agreements would have an objective limited to offsetting further inequalisation—an objective which, with good will and adequate effort, could be given operational form—the North would reduce the risk of unilateral cartelisation and would face a smooth price enhancement process in contrast to the sharp price shocks experienced in the case of oil. The South, in return for accepting a limited objective, would not have to incur the cost of policing a unilateral cartel, would eliminate the risk of retaliation, and would be subject to less uncertainty all round.

(e) *Is there a better way?*

Price enhancement with the limited objective described above would hold steady the distribution of income between North and South in so far as this depends on the pattern of international specialisation. Even so, it may be viewed as a redistributor of income (in comparison with what the market left to itself would have brought about), and clearly as a method for achieving this it is not unique.

Tax-financed aid is favourably contrasted by many authors (e.g. Johnson 1977; Bauer and Yamey 1981)[2] to redistribution by price enhancement. The former is said to be a zero-sum game—the losers losing exactly what the gainers gain—while the latter is a negative-sum game because it carries a deadweight burden.

As a proposition about pure aid—non-repayable, interest-free, stringless, guaranteed to last and free of charity odium—this is valid, though even then its importance is limited when, as shown in section 1 (a) of this chapter, the deadweight burden of price enhancement is small. But in the real world the bulk of bilateral aid (and some multilateral) is politically slanted, is tied to purchases from the donor country and is subject to the uncertainties of the donor country's internal political process. As Bird and Gutman (1981) have put it: 'Research has been singularly unsuccessful in explaining the pattern of aid either in humanitarian or economic terms.' Neither need (as measured by the degree of poverty) nor efficiency (as measured by the rate of return or growth rate) can account for the observed pattern. The Brandt Report (1980) is conscious of the need to depoliticise aid and endorses proposals for automatic revenue raisers such as predetermined rates of levy on international trade, but this is certain to fall on deaf ears for the time being.

A proposal was unfolded at UNCTAD IV in 1976 by the then US Secretary of State, Henry Kissinger, which was intended to trump price enhancement pressures by appearing to do even better than just avoid a deadweight burden. Redistribution was now to take place in the context of a positive-sum game through setting up a bank to finance the exploration and extraction of natural resources in the South: the world would gain from the alleviation of perceived scarcities of natural resources and the developing countries would get a disproportionate share of the gain by obtaining finance on concessionary terms.

The proposal fell flat. Cheaper and more abundant capital for resource extraction will raise output but will also lower prices and in so far as this concerned commodities with globally price-inelastic demand and predominantly produced by developing countries for export, the fall of prices would be in greater proportion than the rise of output, with a negative net effect for the South as a whole.[3]

The perspective gained from viewing developing countries as a whole is important here. From the viewpoint of any one developing country an expansion of output could be beneficial, but its gain would be mainly at the expense of other developing country producers who would carry the lower price consequences of such expansion. And this is not confined to natural resources: the expansion of tea or coffee production in, say, Kenya benefits Kenya but on balance harms developing countries as a whole.

The 'small country' myopia, if excusable in individual developing countries, is entirely inexcusable but very much present in national and international aid agencies; its perpetuation is an incidental but unfortunate by-product of the widespread application to cost benefit analysis of the Little–Mirrlees (1969) practice of valuing inputs and outputs at the going international prices even though the authors warn (pp. 108–9), if rather unemphatically, that it is inappropriate outside price-taker situations.

It is often said (*inter alia* MacBean (1978, p. 23)) that there is a 'liberal' policy alternative which is superior to price-raising restrictive measures in satisfying the aspirations of developing countries: its principal component is the abolition of agricultural protection in developed countries. The superiority of such a policy again rests on the view that it involves a positive-sum game, the net gain for the world as a whole arising from the elimination of the perceived misallocation of resources associated with protection. But quite apart from the fact that the commodities which stand to benefit from such liberalisation are not those which are predominantly produced in developing countries (with the main exception of sugar, there is no protection against these in developed countries), this is not a redistributive idea at all. In terms of the neoclassical analytical apparatus of those who advocate it, the North as a whole stands to gain by such a policy and should be persuaded to institute it for its own sake and not as an alternative to, or as part of a bargain involving the abandonment of, strictly redistributive action.

(f) *Price enhancement by what means?*

In the light of all this it is difficult to see how the alleged superiority of alternatives to price enhancement can be sustained. But, at a lower level of discourse, there is still the question of how best to bring about price enhancement.

There has been much debate on export quotas versus export taxes as a means of effecting price-enhancing supply restrictions. (For yet other ways of effecting price enhancement see Maizels (1976).)

Although quotas are more certain in their operation, many economists favour taxes (*inter alia* Henderson and Lal (1976), Bird (1979)). The strongest arguments for taxes are that they capture the monopoly rents for the general public of the producing countries through the intermediation of (presumed benevolent) governments and that they give more scope for those gaining most in efficiency (within the group of developing countries) to acquire an increasing share.[4] Some combination of taxes and quotas may be politically more acceptable without being inferior in its optimality properties; a scheme by Kaldor (1964) ingeniously combines both.

A third method of price enhancement—by cumulatively stockpiling the excess of unrestricted production—may be dismissed as non-feasible in the long run. (See Behrman and Tinakorn-Ramangkura (1979) for simulation-estimated costs of financing such a scheme.)

The distribution of the benefits from price enhancement among the developing countries themselves has also been a much debated issue. On this suffice to say three things. First, while the incidence of benefits of any single commodity scheme would fall very unevenly among countries, an integrated programme for all the South-dominated commodities for which price enhancement is feasible will spread the benefits very widely. Second, the benefits from a scheme of limited price enhancement, along the lines favoured here, basically offset distributive losses which would have fallen on producing countries if the market was left to itself; the gains would accrue in very large measure to those who would have suffered the losses. Third, some developing countries would nevertheless be virtually untouched, gaining little from price enhancement because they would have lost little in its absence, but among them are numbered some of the very poorest countries in the world and therefore countries entitled to very special attention; that they are peripheral to the concerns of this monograph is just an accident of the subject chosen for treatment.

2. DIVERSIFICATION

Successive price enhancements cannot usefully continue indefinitely. They push consumers to more elastic regions of their demand curves and thus erode their own redistributive effectiveness. (In terms of the model of Chapter V they may also weaken the inequalising effects of traditional specialisation.) Moreover, the output restrictions associated with price enhancement must imply some increase in the already severe unemployment in many developing countries, which may appear counter-intuitive to policy makers, even though the gains from price enhancement are a large multiple of the foregone output of those rendered unemployed by it.

In the long run, a policy of accelerated expansion of sectors of the economy outside traditional primary exportables is called for.[5]

This essentially means either expansion of domestically oriented food production or expansion of manufacturing.

Expansion of domestically oriented food production will be congenial to those who forecast an increasingly negative food balance for the world's poor countries; to those, who like Lipton (1977), favour a small unit, village-oriented development strategy; and to those who think in terms of Lewis's model (1969) which implies that, regardless of anything else, the relative poverty of developing countries will be perpetuated if the productivity of food producers in those countries remains low. From the point of view of this study the relevant consideration is that if the prices of food fall as a result of expanded production and higher productivity, the gainers from the fall are located in the developing countries themselves; there is no dissipation of gains to the rich countries through adverse price movements.

Promotion of manufacturing is now widely (but not unanimously) accepted as a component of development policy. For the present the important point is that, in the absence of direct restrictions on traditional exportables, an increment of manufactures yields a social benefit in excess of the private benefit to the extent that it keeps down those sectors producing traditional exportables which, from the viewpoint of developing countries as a whole, yield a negative marginal product.

Controversy in the trade context centres on whether promotion of manufactures should be import-substituting or export-oriented. This study has no specific contribution at the level of principles to make on this issue. Indeed, the issue is not a matter of principle but a matter of circumstances—for example circumstances of size (Malta or Cyprus cannot gain much mileage from import substitution but India or Brazil can) or circumstances of developmental phase (a country cannot continue to give priority to import substitution indefinitely without encountering projects which are inferior to export-oriented ones).

At the practical level the optical angle of this study, which views the developing countries as a whole, may contribute a special perspective.

Industrialisation projects in developing countries (usually import-substituting ones) which Little, Scitovsky, and Scott (1970, Chapter 5), and Bhagwati and Srinivasan (1975, pp. 177-8) and others have found utterly wasteful, some to the point of showing negative value added when evaluated at (constant) international prices, may have been unjustly maligned by a methodology employing constant prices which is not appropriate from the viewpoint of the welfare of developing countries as a whole.

Cross-sectional studies, such as those of Michaely (1977), Kruger (1978) and Balassa (1978 and more recently 1981a and 1981b), which establish an empirical superiority for an outward-directed (export-promoting) development policy over an inward-directed (import-substituting) one, may be victims of the fallacy of composition in implying that because some of the countries did better through an outward-directed policy, all could do better: they may not, since they would be competing against, and scoring gains off, each other—see Cline (1982).

Of course anybody acquainted with these matters knows of ill-conceived, ill-planned, ill-executed, ill-managed industrialisation projects, and the preceding paragraphs must not be interpreted as denying this. But these things are not unknown in developed countries and the only general moral that may be drawn from them is that, if avoidable, they should be avoided and that if they constitute the cost of 'learning by doing', such cost should be properly allowed for in project selection.

A pessimistic view of industrialisation is implied by Griffin (1974), who hypothesises a continuing deterioration of the DFTT for the manufacturing and primary-producing sectors of developing countries alike. He rests this on the overwhelming concentration of research and innovative effort in the North. By different reasoning Amin (1976, pp. 168-9) arrives at the same hypothesis. Singer (1974-5) and others share the pessimism about industrialisation.

A cursory calculation suggests that the DFTT of developing country manufactures *vis-à-vis* developed country manufactures have indeed deteriorated in the sixties and seventies. But one must not stop there. For there has also been a large expansion of employment in the manufacturing sector of developing countries, enough to compensate for the DFTT deterioration. With unemployed labour in the background and some positive cost attached to productivity increases, it is efficient not to match the productivity growth rate of developed countries but to expand employment instead.

Pronounced expansion of manufacturing in developing countries will keep pressing down the relative prices of manufactures in developed countries and in so doing will counter the inequalising effects of traditional specialisation. But, by the time this counter-influence comes to dominate, if it does, the share of primary exportables in the developing countries' output and trade might have fallen to the point where it would not matter very much whether the traditional specialisation had inequalising effects or not.

3. CONCLUSION AND SUMMARY

The inequalising effects which the traditional pattern of specialisation has on developing countries, as revealed in this book, could be stemmed by collectively enforced successive price enhancements for a number of South-dominated commodities.

It could be unwise for developed countries to oppose participation in a price-enhancing scheme limited to the prevention of further inequalisation. While developing countries at present lack sufficient cohesion to enforce price enhancement unilaterally, no other conditions for a successful cartelisation can be confidently said to fail. Developed countries, though not immediately haunted by 'commodity power', could find that to rely persistently on the absence of cohesion may itself provoke cohesion as a reaction and, anyway, in the light of OPEC history it should not come as a surprise if cohesion-cementing circumstances were to arise suddenly for seemingly extraneous reasons.

Moreover, the alleged allocative inefficiency of price-enhancing schemes is too insubstantial to carry any weight, while the redistributive alternatives to price enhancement sometimes proposed do not possess the robust superiority claimed for them.

In the longer run developing countries need a policy of accelerated diversification into manufacturing and/or domestically oriented food production to bring about a more rapid erosion of the traditional pattern of specialisation and its inequalising effects.

NOTES

CHAPTER I

[1] Textbooks do show that when one trading partner is small and the other large, while prices are competitively determined, the small partner gains most. But the South is not small in the relevant sense, nor are the business enterprises or the trade unions of the North devoid of market power.

[2] Cooper (1977) and others deny even the possibility of impoverishment by trade, but only by neglecting historical locking-in and also market failure.

[3] The work of Hughes and Singh (1978) and of Yeats (1981, Chapter 2) may, however, provide alternative routes to the quantification of exchange inequality. See also Gibson (1980).

[4] The validity of this conclusion depends on the income elasticity of demand for the performing arts not exceeding unity by an amount sufficient to compensate for the relative price rise.

[5] Of course when synthetic fibres and beet sugar were in their very expansionary phases, they were making things more difficult, not less, for cotton and cane sugar. But remember that the data on which the findings are based are for the period 1960–77.

[6] Strictly, a price elasticity less than infinite suffices to bring about some suboptimality, but for the loss to be substantial elasticities must be low. (For illustrative calculations see Johnson (1968).) Note that this is not a once-over phenomenon, as may be seen by the fact that if initially there was an optimum tariff/tax, it would have to be raised each time new productivity growth opportunities presented themselves to avert an *ex post* socially excessive rise of output. In optimum tariff theory it is well known that growth typically undermines the optimality of a given tariff rate—see Bhagwati (1968, 1973).

CHAPTER II

[1] Singer (1958) shifted to the position that what deteriorates is not the NBTT of primary products but the NBTT of developing countries regardless of what they export—a position which he has more recently reiterated (1974–5) and broadened.

[2] The interesting model which Bacha (1978) calls the 'Prebisch-Singer model' can be so called only by poetic licence since it assumes monopolistic pricing of the Periphery's product.

[3] But note that more recently Kaldor (1976) confines the role of price formation asymmetry to shorter-run adjustment phenomena, a subject which will be taken up in section 2.

[4] However, the reverse also occurs. Dasgupta (1974, p. 111) writes that 'exponents of the Prebisch thesis usually attribute the decline to low-income elasticity of demand for primary goods . . . and to technical change leading to a substitution of natural raw materials by synthetics . . .' but says nothing about asymmetrical price formation.

[5] There are of course writings, both critical and supportive, which take a broader view of the Prebisch–Singer hypothesis, *inter alia* Baer (1969), Flanders (1964), and Hyde (1963).

[6] When $w_c \equiv$ initial share of primary output in total output, the percentage increase in world real income at an unchanged relative price is $w_c\dot{\Pi}_c + (1 - w_c)\dot{\Pi}^*_m$, whence the percentage increase in demand for C is $\epsilon^g_c\{w_c\dot{\Pi}_c + (1 - w_c)\dot{\Pi}^*_m\}$. The percentage increase in primary supply is $\dot{\Pi}_c$. Therefore, at an unchanged relative price, the excess demand for C in percentage terms $= \epsilon^g_c\{w_c\dot{\Pi}_c + (1 - w_c)\dot{\Pi}^*_m\} - \dot{\Pi}_c$, whence it follows that the NBTT (which will respond to excess demand) will improve, remain constant or deteriorate according as

$$\epsilon^g_c \gtreqless \frac{\dot{\Pi}_c}{w_c\dot{\Pi}_c + (1 - w_c)\dot{\Pi}^*_m} \qquad \text{(II.1)}$$

A corresponding excess demand equation for manufactures would yield the condition that the NBTT for primary products will improve, remain constant or deteriorate according as

$$\epsilon^g_m \lesseqgtr \frac{\dot{\Pi}^*_m}{w_c\dot{\Pi}_c + (1 - w_c)\dot{\Pi}^*_m}. \qquad \text{(II.2)}$$

The two excess demand equations are not independent and (II.2) can be derived from (II.1) by using the identity $w_c\epsilon^g_c + (1 - w_c)\epsilon^g_m \equiv 1$. By combining (II.1) and (II.2) we obtain the condition in the form given in the text.

[7] As examples of recent papers which incorporate both the assumption and the result see Bacha (1978) and Findlay (1979). For a discussion of the assumptions underlying an infinite elasticity of labour supply see Chapter V, section 5.

[8] This follows from the fact that P_cC/P_m gives the volume of M for which a given volume of C will exchange. When this is constant $\log(P_c/P_m) + \log C =$ constant, which is the equation of a line such as $\overline{Y}\overline{Y}$ in the diagram.

[9] For example, Pincus (1967, p. 131) refers to 'The Prebisch–Singer–Myrdal view'. As a footnote to the history of ideas it is interesting to note that all three were distinguished servants of the UN when the

terms of trade thesis was being developed: Prebisch headed the Economic Commission for Latin America in Santiago, Singer was at the UN Secretariat in New York, and Myrdal headed the Economic Commission for Europe in Geneva.

[10] See his carefully and sometimes non-commitally worded expositions in Myrdal (1956a, p. 49; 1956b, p. 232; 1968, pp. 610–11). In Myrdal (1970) he states categorically that 'the trading position of most underdeveloped countries in the post-colonial era has deteriorated and probably will continue to deteriorate', but supports this with the observed decrease in the share in world trade of traditional exports from developing countries, while saying nothing about terms of trade.

[11] At an unchanged relative price,

$$\text{the percentage increase in primary supply} = \dot{\Pi}_c + e_c\dot{\Pi}_c.$$

The first right-hand term accounts for the increase in supply at the initial level of employment; the second term for the increase due to additional employment associated with a higher real wage—higher by the increase in Π_c, since the relative price of C is assumed unchanged. Given the technology, output increases by the same percentage as employment.

Still at an unchanged relative price,

$$\text{the percentage increase in world real income} = w_c\dot{\Pi}_c + (1 - w_c)\dot{\Pi}^*_m + w_c e_c\dot{\Pi}_c.$$

The first two right-hand terms represent the weighted average increase of output attributable to the initial labour force and the third term the increase due to additional employment (the proportionate weight of which is governed by w_c).

The percentage increase in the demand for C is equal to the percentage increase in world income multiplied by income elasticity ϵ_c. Hence, always at an unchanged relative price, the excess demand for C in percentage terms =

$$\epsilon^g_c\{w_c\dot{\Pi}_c + (1 - w_c)\dot{\Pi}^*_m + w_c e_c\dot{\Pi}_c\} - (\dot{\Pi}_c + e_c\dot{\Pi}_c).$$

When it is assumed that $\epsilon^g_c = 1$, the result reported in the text follows.

[12] In keeping with the assumptions of Emmanuel, Amin, and other unequal exchange exponents, let capital and labour be the inputs and let capital mobility equalise profit rates. If then it is assumed that the capital/output ratio is the same at home and abroad, the wages in both countries will bear the same proportion to output per person valued at the ruling price, i.e. $W/P_i\Pi = W^*/P_j\Pi^*$ where $W \equiv$ wage, $P \equiv$ price and the asterisk denotes symbols appertaining to the foreign country. Since unequal exchange in the Amin sense occurs when $W/\Pi \neq W^*/\Pi^*$,

it implies $P_i \neq P_j$. But this is impossible in a market economy when i and j are identical goods (abstracting from tariffs, transport costs, and other impediments to trade). (The dual of this is that if $P_i = P_j$, the assumption of profit rate equalisation must be violated. Cf. de Janvry and Kramer (1979).) If i and j are not identical, $P_i \neq P_j$ is possible but devoid of meaning.

If the equality of capital/output ratios is discarded, i and j can be identical goods (so that $P_i = P_j$) consistently with $W/\Pi \neq W^*/\Pi^*$, but in that case the country with the lower capital/output ratio will have the higher wage relatively to productivity. (Remember that profit rates are equalised through capital mobility.) Since the capital/output ratio would be expected to be lower in poor countries, the beneficiaries of unequal exchange would be the poor countries!

[13] Nothing is affected if, instead of zero barriers, constant barriers to trade are postulated, meaning that they are such as to make the price of F in one region a constant fraction of the price of F in the other region.

CHAPTER III

[1] Though Prebisch did not recognise this, it is implied by his arguments. In keeping with these, one would have expected him to contend that primary products predominantly produced by developed countries need not share the fate of deteriorating relative price *vis-à-vis* manufactures, for either of two reasons: (i) because workers are unionised in primary production as well as manufactures, if only less intensively; and/or (ii) because there is alternative secondary and tertiary employment to which they can and do transfer, thus relieving the supply pressure on the price of primary products. (See also introductory section of Chapter II.)

[2] Those of Schlote (1952) and the Board of Trade, as given in UN (1949, Table 5).

[3] It is an interesting fact, perhaps not widely known because of the anonymity of UN staff publications, that the principal author was Hans Singer who became the second twin in the 'Prebisch–Singer thesis' through a subsequent signed article (1950).

[4] For reasons indicated in the last paragraph of the introductory section no weight would be attached to a possible objection that there is an obvious non-linearity in these series which the above regressions fail to capture. But it may be reported as a footnote that all the simple regressions of NBTT on t reported in this section were extended to include t^2 also as a regressor. The effect in most cases was to improve R^2 negligibly, to render the coefficient of t insignificant at the 5 per cent level and to yield a coefficient of t^2 negative and significant. The negative relation with time was therefore unchanged.

[5] As indicated in the notes to Table III.1, the League series uses the Sauerbeck index as proxy for the price of traded primary products. More recently Ray (1977) has used *The Economist* index which also goes back a long way. The Sauerbeck index was the unweighted average of prices for 37 commodities (some of the more important commodities being given implicitly a larger weight by being represented by prices for more than one type or grade) as against *The Economist* index which down to 1911 was the unweighted average of prices of 22 commodities. (In 1911 *The Economist* index was extended to 44 commodities and in 1927 to 58. In 1924 it switched to geometric averaging.) For the forty years 1871–1910 the two indices slowly diverged, *The Economist* index showing a price fall between the two end-years of some 10 per cent as against some 20 per cent shown by the Sauerbeck index.

[6] From Maizels (1963, p. 88) it is possible to construct the following ratio for selected years: unit value of total exports of countries other than those defined as industrial ÷ unit value of exports of manufactures of industrial countries. (The industrial countries are Belgium-Luxembourg, Canada, France, Germany, Italy, Japan, Netherlands, Sweden, Switzerland, UK, and US.) The values obtained are: 1899, 81; 1913, 100; 1929, 86; 1937, 80.

[7] For alternative ways of splicing different series, see Barratt Brown (1974, pp. 246–51).

[8] The World Bank does, however, deviate a little from the UN's list of countries deemed to be developing.

[9] This can be seen by extending to post-war the NBTT index of note 6, which was constructed from data to be found in Maizels (1963, p. 88): 1950, 150; 1955, 122; 1957, 115; 159, 107.

[10] This can be inferred, with all the appropriate reservations, from the terms of trade series for the UK compiled by Imlah (1950).

CHAPTER IV

[1] All these authors concern themselves with SFTT. Constantopoulos and Drakos (1981) do so also but in a modified form. Kindleberger (1956) has had a shot at estimating DFTT for which he disclaimed, however, anything more than an illustrative role. He used labour productivity.

[2] For the relation between total factor productivity indices and statistical production functions of neoclassical inspiration see Kendrick (1973, pp. 11–15). For a wide-ranging review of productivity research with the emphasis on total productivity see Nadiri (1970). Fabricant's (1974) survey introduces some scepticism while Nelson's (1981) is markedly critical of neoclassically based work on total productivity.

[3] Balanced trade is not a very restrictive condition if the current account deficit is financed by debt incurred on commerical terms for then, under certain assumptions, the discounted present value of the future export surplus required to discharge the debt would be equal to the increment of present-day exports which would have bridged the deficit.

[4] Viner (1937, p. 563) had proposed a formula for what he called the 'total gain from trade', which was similar to the ITT, except that X stood for the 'volume of trade', an ambiguous term for which Viner offered no definition. Staehle (1951) assumed that it meant the volume of exports, in which case Viner's concept is identical to the ITT, while Imlah (1950) took it for granted that it meant the sum of imports and exports. Under a variety of names, such as 'capacity to import' or 'purchasing power of exports', ITT series are now widely computed, mostly by international organisations (for the most extensive effort see UNCTAD (1979)), but also by academic researchers (see Wilson *et al.* (1969)).

[5] Thanks are due to Geoffrey Heal who, by working out the explicit mathematics of this, cleared up a confusion concerning the case of non-unity-elastic demand.

[6] With positive but constant marginal cost of extraction, the rate of NBTT improvement needed to compensate for resource depletion will be slower the higher the initial share of marginal cost in price, because it is only the royalty component of price which needs to rise. If the marginal cost of extraction rises, the needed rate of improvement of the NBTT is faster the steeper the rise in marginal cost because otherwise the royalty component would be eroded.

CHAPTER V

[1] This distances the present model from 'steady state' methodology which virtually imposes unity income elasticity, as for example in Findlay (1980).

[2] A compendium of available elasticity estimates for agricultural commodities can be found in World Bank (1980). The World Bank's own working assumptions about elasticities, including those of minerals, are reported in World Bank (1975). Labys (1978) gives a bibliographic list of 337 commodity models.

[3] The large 'unexplained' residual in attempts such as Denison's (1967) to 'explain' the historical growth of productivity may reflect this fact but does not exhaust it. For the growth of the capital stock, which accounts for much of the 'explained' part in, for example, Jorgenson and Griliches (1967), cannot be sensibly viewed as determined

by the supply of savings alone and hence independently of the micro-competition which generates embodied technical progress. Similar observations apply to other explanatory variables such as Research and Development.

[4] While capital does not enter explicitly, it is well known that the relation embodied in (V.1) and (V.2) is consistent with capital being and input under more than one set of assumptions—for example, if technical progress is neutral, and the capital/labour ratio is constant. Thus if K is capital and θ is a measure of exogenous technical progress, there are subclasses of the production function $S = \theta f(K, N)$ which may be linearly approximated by $S = \theta N \times$ a constant if K/N is constant. Whence $S = \Pi N$, where $\Pi \equiv \theta \times$ a constant. If N is growing it has to be assumed, in order to ensure macroeconomic equilibrium, that savings adjust in such a way that the growth of K can keep in step with the growth of N, which is what happens also in neoclassical growth models in the 'steady state'. At least one good in the model must serve as a capital as well as a consumption good. Under a constant rate of output growth, the part of demand attributable to investment will grow in proportion to output in each country.

[5] By differentiating logarithmically and solving, while bearing in mind the restriction that the price-weighted sum of commodities and manufactures demanded must equal world income.

[6] The empirical evidence of price inelasticity relates to Marshallian 'own price' elasticities, whereas at present a substitution elasticity is being used. But, as may be seen by exploring the implication of (V.12), the results obtained hold equally for 'own price' elasticities.

[7] It measures real income on the assumption that only imported manufactures are consumed in that sector. This assumption captures in a stylised fashion the fact that developing countries retain a small fraction of their own major primary exportables while finding it difficult to extract a surplus from the primitive sector to sustain a growing labour force in the modern sector. In the notation of Chapter IV this is the special case in which $\omega = 1$. The condition $\omega + \omega^* = 1$ (which is needed to make the ECDFTT an accurate index of inequalisation—see section 4 of Chapter IV) is then satisfied if $\omega^* = 0$, which is not so far-fetched since, as it happens, less than 10 per cent of the North's manufacturing output is exported to the South. The model allows for incremental consumption of its own exportables by Southland as its income expands.

[8] This can be seen as follows. Reformulate (V.13) to read

$$N_c = \Phi(R)$$

where $R \equiv$ ratio of average earnings in Southland's two sectors $\equiv P\Pi_c \div \bar{Q}/(N - N_c)$. $\bar{Q} \equiv$ constant output of primitive sector. Differentiate logarithmically

$$\dot{N}_c = \frac{\nu_c'}{1 + \dfrac{N_c}{N - N_c}\,\nu_c'}\,(\dot{P} + \dot{\Pi}_c)$$

where $\nu_c' \equiv R\partial\Phi/N_c\partial R$. Perfect mobility is represented by $\nu_c' = \infty$ and it is evident that

$$\lim_{\nu_c' \to \infty}\left(\frac{\nu_c'}{1 + \dfrac{N_c}{N - N_c}\,\nu_c'}\right) = \frac{N - N_c}{N_c}.$$

[9] On the other hand, conditions for ECDFTT deterioration are less stringent than the deterioration of the SFTT. By definition Southland's SFTT $\equiv P\Pi_c$, therefore $\overset{\bullet}{\overbrace{\text{SFTT}}} = \dot{P} + \dot{\Pi}_c = \overset{\bullet}{\overbrace{\text{DFTT}}} + \dot{\Pi}_m^*$. Since $0 < \nu_c/(1 + \nu_c) \leqslant 1$, the ECDFTT may fail to improve when the SFTT improve, but not vice versa.

[10] This may be shown in the following way. Differentiate logarithmically (V.18) and (V.19):

$$\dot{N}_c^* = \nu_c^*(\dot{P} + \dot{\Pi}_c^* - \dot{\Pi}_m^*)$$
$$\dot{\Pi}_c^* = \dot{\bar{\Pi}}_c^* - \beta\dot{N}_c^*.$$

Combine these two expressions to obtain

$$\dot{N}_c^* = \frac{\nu_c^*}{1 + \beta\nu_c^*}\,(\dot{P} + \dot{\bar{\Pi}}_c^* - \dot{\Pi}_m^*).$$

It now follows that under perfect mobility between sectors

$$\lim_{\nu_c^* \to \infty}\left(\frac{\nu_c^*}{1 + \beta\nu_c^*}\right) = \frac{1}{\beta}.$$

[11] Given the (conventional) restrictions on signs of coefficients as already indicated, namely $\epsilon_c^g \geqslant 0$, $\nu_c \geqslant 0$, $0 \leqslant w_c^g \leqslant 1$, $0 < \beta < 1$, and $(\eta_c^g + w_c^g\epsilon_c^g) \equiv$ income-compensated price elasticity < 0.

[12] This assertion depends on the assumption that $\dot{\bar{\Pi}}_c^* = \dot{\Pi}_c$, which was used to arrive at (V.21). If $\dot{\bar{\Pi}}_c^* > \dot{\Pi}_c$, the deterioration presumption is strengthened further but if $\dot{\bar{\Pi}}_c^* < \dot{\Pi}_c$, it is not strengthened as much.

CHAPTER VI

[1] Additionally, minerals tend to have higher income elasticities than agricultural commodities, though typically still on the nether side of unity.

[2] SITC classes 67 and 68 which are included in the value of mineral exports contain refining and fabrication elements. Since there has been an expansion of downstream processing in the producing countries, the growth in mineral exports is exaggerated by a disproportionately growing manufacturing component. But if these classes were excluded there would be a downward bias from the failure to capture minerals which, having ceased to be exported in crude form, are exported none the less.

[3] As against 10 to 30 per cent retained of the other four commodities.

[4] The World Bank's index for twenty-six agricultural commodities weighted by their importance in developing country exports, when regressed on time, yielded a coefficient of −0.0060 with *T*-ratio = −1.556.

[5] Kravis and Lipsey (1977 and 1978) assembled some data which bear on the legitimacy of such procedure.

[6] The alternative index is as follows:

Employment-deflated manufacturing GDP of developed market economies at current prices*
1970 = 100

Year	1960	'61	'62	'63	'64	'65	'66	'67	'68	'69	'70
Index number	57	57	61	64	70	74	78	81	88	95	100

Year	'71	'72	'73	'74	'75	'76
Index number	110	126	149	161	179	198

Sources: For manufacturing GDP in national currencies, OECD, *National Accounts 1960–1977*; for exchange rates used to convert to a common currency, International Monetary Fund, *International Financial statistics* (various issues), and for the employment deflator, UN, *Yearbook of Industrial Statistics* (various issues) and UN, *Monthly Bulletin of Statistics* (August 1979).

*The following countries are included: Australia, Austria, Belgium,

Canada, Finland, France, Federal Republic of Germany, Greece, Italy, Japan, Norway, Portugal, Sweden, UK, and US.

[7] The *T*-ratios exceed so comfortably the 5 per cent significance borderline that the presence of auto-correlation (as revealed by the Durbin-Watson statistic) in some of the cases does not vitiate the statistical significance of the results.

[8] Or so one may deduce from the fact that in seventeen developed countries grouped together, the annual gross investment/value added ratio in manufacturing was completely trendless over the period 1963-74: highest at 0.177 in 1970 and lowest at 0.154 in 1963. The countries were Australia, Belgium, Canada, Denmark, Finland, France, Federal Republic of Germany, Greece, Ireland, Japan, Netherlands, Norway, Portugal, South Africa, Sweden, UK, and US. Data in national currencies were obtained from UN, *Yearbook of National Accounts Statistics* (various issues) and UN, *Yearbook of Industrial Statistics* (various issues) and for purposes of aggregation were converted to a common currency by using exchange rates from IMF, *International Financial Statistics* (various issues).

[9] Output per head of population grew more slowly in developing than developed countries, but inequalisation due to demographic or social factors affecting the ratio of economically active to total population, though important in other contexts, is not material to the concerns of this monograph.

CHAPTER VII

[1] ISIC 37 includes products which are subjected to a degree of fabrication that would disqualify them as primary. But in developing countries the bulk of activities included in class 37 consist of metal refining and pig-iron production, the products of which, when exported, are deemed to be primary exports and indeed constitute the major part of primary metal exports of developing countries.

[2] One of a number of inconsistencies arises because P is export weighted while Π_c and Π_m^* are production weighted. But this is mitigated by the fact that in developing countries a substantial proportion of metal production is exported and that for OECD countries the export unit value index and the implicit deflator for manufactures have not diverged significantly over the entire period 1966-77. The problem of inconsistencies between SITC and ISIC groupings is, of course, a perennial one.

CHAPTER VIII

[1] Note that with the pre-cartel output of rivals still Q_{r0}, but the linear MC_r curve more elastic in the neighbourhood of P_{c0} (whence the D_k curve also more elastic), the profit increase associated with the pre-emption strategy will be greater. This follows from the fact that while the position of *A* will not change, that of *B* will move towards the south-west. So the elasticity of the rival's supply curve does play a role after all, not however in constraining the cartel's price-enhancing power but in affecting the incentive for the cartel to engage in self-defence: the higher the elasticity of the rival's supply curve the greater the incentive.

[2] In the case of Bauer and Yamey it is the lesser of two evils because they are opposed to both.

[3] More recently developing countries have been pressing for the creation of a World Bank energy affiliate while the US opposed it. Energy is a special case in that cartelisation has already brought about a dramatic rise in petroleum prices and the petroleum-producing countries are interested in ways of relieving the burden on petroleum-importing developing countries. The US opposition was doctrinal: it preferred to leave the area to private capital.

[4] Flexibility in quota provisions, as provided for in some international commodity agreements, can also go some way towards the latter objective. See Maizels (1981).

[5] Except in so far as developing countries have a small share in some of these primary exportables, in which event they could expand them by displacing developed country output without adverse terms of trade effects if the prospect of such displacement did not trigger off increased protection.

REFERENCES

Abramovitz, M. (1956) 'Resource and Output Trends in the United States Since 1870', *American Economic Review*, Vol. 46 (May), pp. 5–23.

Amin, S. (1976) *Unequal Development*, Sussex, England, Harvester Press.

Anell, L. and Nygren, B. (1980) *The Developing Countries and the World Economic Order*, London, Frances Pinter.

Angermann, O. (1980) 'External Terms of Trade of the Federal Republic of Germany Using Different Methods of Deflation', *Review of Income and Wealth*, Vol. 26, pp. 367–85.

Appleyard, D. R. (1974) 'Factor Productivity and the Gains from Trade: An Estimate of India's Single Factorial Terms of Trade', *Indian Economic Journal*, Vol. 22, pp. 36–49.

Auer, L. (1969) *Canadian Agricultural Productivity*, Staff Study No. 24, Economic Council of Canda.

Bacha, E. L. (1978) 'An Interpretation of Unequal Exchange from Prebisch to Emmanuel', *Journal of Development Economics*, Vol. 5, pp. 319–30.

Baer, W. (1969) 'The Economics of Prebisch and ECLA', in C. T. Nisbet (ed.), *Problems of Economic Development*, New York, Free Press, pp. 203–18.

Bairoch, P. (1975) *The Economic Development of the Third World Since 1900*, London, Methuen.

Balassa, B. (1978) 'Exports and Economic Growth: Further Evidence', *Journal of Development Economics*, Vol. 5, pp. 181–9.

Balassa, B. (1981a) *The Policy Experience of Twelve Less Developed Countries, 1973–78*, Staff Working Paper No. 449, World Bank.

Balassa, B. (1981b) 'Adjustment to External Shocks in Developing Economies', Staff Working Paper No. 472, World Bank.

Baldwin, R. E. (1955) 'Secular Movements in the Terms of Trade', *American Economic Review, Papers and Proceedings*, Vol. 45 (May), pp. 259–69.

Baldwin, R. E. (1966) *Economic Development and Growth*, New York, John Wiley.

Barratt Brown, M. (1974) *The Economics of Imperialism*, Harmondsworth, Middlesex, Penguin.

Bauer, P. T. and Yamey, B. (1981) 'The Political Economy of Foreign Aid', *Lloyds Bank Review*, (Oct.) pp. 1–14.

Baumol, W. J. and Bowen, W. G. (1965) 'On the Performing Arts:

The Antomy of Their Economic Problems', *American Economic Review*, Vol. 55 (May), pp. 495-502.

Behrman, J. R. and Tinakorn-Ramangkura, P. (1979) 'Indexation of International Commodity Prices Through International Buffer Stock Operations', *Journal of Policy Modelling*, Vol. 1, pp. 113-34.

Bell, R. T. (1979) 'Theories of the Terms of Trade of Less Developed Countries: A Critical Survey', *Economia Internazionale*, Vol. 32, pp. 200-17.

Bhagwati, J. (1957-8) 'Immiserizing Growth: A Geometric Note', *Review of Economic Studies*, Vol. 25, pp. 201-5.

Bhagwati, J. (1958) 'International Trade and Economic Expansion', *American Economic Review*, Vol. 48, pp. 941-53.

Bhagwati, J. (1968) 'Distortions and Immiserizing Growth: A Generalisation', *Review of Economic Studies*, Vol. 35, pp. 481-5.

Bhagwati, J. (1973) 'The Theory of Immiserizing Growth: Further Applications', in A. K. Connolly and A. Swoboda (eds), *International Trade and Money*, London, Allen & Unwin.

Bhagwati, J. and Srinivasan, T. N. (1975) *Foreign Trade Regimes and Economic Development*, India, New York, and London, Columbia University Press for the National Bureau of Economic Research.

Bird, G. (1979) 'The Terms of Trade of Developing Countries: Theory, Evidence and Policy', *Economia Internazionale*, Vol. 32, pp. 399-413.

Bird, G. and Gutman, P. (1981) 'Foreign Aid—The Issues', *National Westminster Bank Quarterly Review*, (Aug.), pp. 36-51.

Bloomfield, A. I. (1981) 'Miscellany: An Early Anticipation of the Concept of Immiserizing Growth', *Journal of International Economics*, Vol. 11, pp. 423-7.

Brandt, W. (Chairman) (1980) *North-South: A Programme for Survival* (Report of the Independent Commission on International Development Issues), London and Sydney, Pan Books.

Bukharin, N. (1930) *Imperialism and World Economy* (written in 1915), London, Martin Lawrence.

Cardoso, F. H. (1977) 'The Originality of a Copy: CEPAL and the Idea of Development', *CEPAL Review*, UN, ECLA, Vol. 4, pp. 7-40.

Caves, R. E. and Porter, M. E. (1977) 'From Entry Barriers to Mobility Barriers: Conjectural Decisions and Contrived Deterrence to New Competition', *Quarterly Journal of Economics*, Vol. 91, pp. 241-61.

Chichilnisky, G. (1981) 'Terms of Trade and Domestic Distribution: Export-Led Growth with Abundant Labour', *Journal of Development Economics*, Vol. 8, pp. 163-92.

Clark, C. (1942) *The Economics of 1960*, London, Macmillan.

Cline, W. R. (1980) 'Commodity Prices and the World Distribution of Income', *Journal of Policy Modelling*, Vol. 2, pp. 1-17.

Cline, W. R. (1981) 'Real Economic Effects of World Inflation and Recession', in W. R. Cline and Associates, *World Inflation and the Developing Countries,* Washington DC, Brookings Institution.

Cline, W. R. (1982) 'Can the East Asian Model of Development be Generalised?', *World Development,* Vol. 10, pp. 81-90.

Commonwealth Secretariat (1975) *Terms of Trade for Primary Commodities,* study directed by J. P. Hayes, London.

Constantopoulos, M. and Drakos, G. E. (1981) 'Welfare Effects of Changes in the Terms of Trade in a Country with a Large Balance of Trade Deficit: The Case of Greece 1960–1980', paper presented to the conference of the International Economic Association in Athens, 31 August-5 September 1981.

Cooper, R. N. (1977) 'A New International Economic Order for Mutual Gain', *Foreign Policy,* No. 26, pp. 66-120.

Cuddy, J. D. A. (1976) *International Price Indexation*, Farnborough, England, and Lexington, Mass., U.S., Saxon House/Lexington Books.

Dadone, A. A. and Di Marco, L. E. (1972) 'The Impact of Prebisch's Ideas on Modern Economic Analysis', in L. E. di Marco (ed.), *International Economics and Development: Essays in Honor of Raul Prebisch,* New York and London, Academic Press, pp. 15–34.

Dasgupta, A. K. (1974) *Economic Theory and the Developing Countries,* London, Macmillan.

De Figueroa, E. (1969) 'La Détérioration des Termes de l'Echange dans les Pays Sous-developpés', *Economie Appliquée,* Vol. 22, pp. 127–52.

De Janvry, A. and Kramer, F. (1979) 'The Limits of Unequal Exchange', *Review of Radical Political Economics*, Vol. 11 (Winter), pp. 3–15.

Denison, E. F. (1967) *Why Growth Rates Differ: Postwar Experience in Nine Western Countries,* Washington DC, Brookings Institution.

Devons, E. (1954) 'Statistics of United Kingdom Terms of Trade', *Manchester School of Economic and Social Studies,* Vol. 22, pp. 258–75.

Diaz-Alejandro, C. F. (1978) 'Delinking North and South: Unshackled or Unhinged?', in A. Fishlow *et al., Rich and Poor Nations in the World Economy,* New York, McGraw Hill for the Council on Foreign Relations, pp. 87–162.

Di Marco, L. E. (1972) 'The Evolution of Prebisch's Economic Thought', in L. E. Di Marco (ed.), *International Economics and Development: Essays in Honour of Raul Prebisch*, New York and London, Academic Press, pp. 3–13.

Dixit, A. (1979) 'A Model of Duopoly Suggesting a Theory of Entry Barriers', *Bell Journal of Economics*, Vol. 10, pp. 20–32.

Domar, E. D. (1962) 'On Total Productivity and All That', *Journal of Political Economy,* Vol. 70, pp. 597-608.

Dorrance, G. S. (1949–50) 'The Income Terms of Trade', *Review of Economic Studies*, Vol. 16, pp. 50–66.

Eaton, B. S. and Lipsey, R. G. (1979) 'The Theory of Market Pre-emption: The Persistence of Excess Capacity and Monopoly in Growing Spatial Markets', *Economica,* Vol. 46, pp. 149–58.

Ellsworth, P. T. (1956) 'The Terms of Trade Between Primary-Producing and Industrial Countries', *Inter-American Economic Affairs,* Vol. 10, pp. 47–65.

Emmanuel, A. (1972) *Unequal Exchange,* New York and London, Monthly Review Press.

Emmanuel, A. (1979) 'The Dynamics of Unequal Exchange/Unequal Development', paper presented to the ELEMEP Conference on Dependency, in March 1979 at the London School of Economics.

Enke, S. (1963) *Economics for Development,* Englewood Cliffs, NJ, Prentice Hall.

Fabricant, S. (1974) 'Perspective on Productivity Research', *Review of Income and Wealth*, Vol. 20, pp. 235–49.

Findlay, R. (1979) 'Economic Development and the Theory of International Trade', *American Economic Review,* Vol. 69 (May), pp. 186–90.

Findlay, R. (1980) 'The Terms of Trade and Equilibrium Growth in the World Economy', *American Economic Review*, Vol. 70, pp. 291–9.

Findlay, R. (1981) 'The Fundamental Determinants of the Terms of Trade', in S. Grassman and E. Lundberg (eds), *The World Economic Order: Past and Prospects,* London and Basingstoke, Macmillan, pp. 425–63.

Flanders, M. J. (1964) 'Prebisch on Protectionism: An Evaluation', *Economic Journal,* Vol. 74, pp. 305–26.

Frank, I. (1976) 'Toward a New Framework for International Commodity Policy', *Finance and Development*, Vol. 13 (June), pp. 17–20.

Gibson, B. (1980) 'Unequal Exchange: Theoretical Issues and Empirical Findings', *Review of Radical Political Economics,* Vol. 12 (Fall), pp. 15–35.

Gilbert, R. J. and Goldman, S. M. (1978) 'Potential Competition and the Monopoly Pricing of an Exhaustible Resource', *Journal of Economic Theory*, Vol. 17, pp. 319–31.

Griffin, K. (1974) 'The International Transmission of Inequality', *World Development,* Vol. 2, pp. 3–15.

Haberler, G. (1936) *Theory of International Trade,* London, Edinburgh and Glasgow, Hodge.

Haberler, G. (1959) *International Trade and Economic Development*, Cairo, National Bank of Egypt.

Haberler, G. (1961) 'Terms of Trade and Economic Development', in H. Ellis (ed.), *Economic Development of Latin America,* New York, St. Martin's Press, pp. 275–97.

Haberler, G. (1964) 'An Assessment of the Current Relevance of the Theory of Production and Trade', *International Journal of Agrarian Affairs,* Vol. 4, pp. 130–49.

Hagen, E. E. (1968) *The Economic of Development,* Homewood, Ill., Irwin.

Harberger, A. C. (1957) 'Some Evidence on the International Price Mechanism', *Journal of Political Economy,* Vol. 65, pp. 506–21.

Heady, C. J. (1981) 'Alternative Theories of Wages in Less Developed Countries: An Empirical Test', paper presented to the SSRC Development Economics Study Group on 27 November 1981.

Helleiner, G. K. (1980) *International Economic Disorder: Essays in North-South Relations,* London and Basingstoke, Macmillan.

Henderson, P. D. and Lal, D. (1976) 'UNCTAD IV, the Commodities Problem and International Economic Reform', *ODI Review,* No. 2, pp. 11–30.

Hicks, J. R. (1953) 'Inaugural Lecture', *Oxford Economic Papers,* Vol. 5, pp. 117–35.

Hotelling, H. (1931) 'The Economics of Exhaustible Resources', *Journal of Political Economy,* Vol. 39, pp. 137–75.

Hughes, H. and Singh, S. (1978) 'Economic Rent: Incidence in Selected Metals and Minerals', *Resources Policy,* Vol. 4, 135–45.

Hyde, F. L. (1963) 'A Critique of the Prebisch Thesis', *Economia Internazionale,* Vol. 16, pp. 463–87.

Imlah, A. H. (1950) 'The Terms of Trade of the United Kingdom 1798–1913', *Journal of Economic History,* Vol. 10, pp. 170–94.

Isserlis, L. (1938) 'Tramp Shipping Cargoes and Freights', *Journal of the Royal Statistical Society,* Vol. 101, pp. 53–146.

Johnson, H. G. (1955) 'Economic Expansion and International Trade', *Manchester School of Economic and Social Studies,* Vol. 23, pp. 95–112.

Johnson, H. G. (1959) 'Economic Development and International Trade', *Nationaløkonomisk Tidsskrift,* Vol. 97, pp. 253–72.

Johnson, H. G. (1967) *Economic Policies Toward Less Developed Countries,* Washington DC, Brookings Institution.

Johnson, H. G. (1968) 'The Gains from Exploiting Monopoly or Monopsony Power in International Trade', *Economica,* Vol. 35, pp. 151–6.

Johnson, H. G. (1977) 'Commodities: Less Developed Countries' Demands and Developed Countries' Responses', in J. Bhagwati (ed.), *The New International Economic Order: The North–South Dialogue,* Cambridge, Mass. and London, MIT Press.

Johnston, B. F. and Tolley, G. S. (1965) 'Strategy for Agriculture in Development', *Journal of Farm Economics,* Vol. 47, pp. 365-79.

Jorgenson, D. W. and Griliches, Z. (1967) 'The Explanation of Productivity Change', *Review of Economic Studies,* Vol. 34, pp. 249-83.

Kaldor, N. (1964) 'Stabilizing the Terms of Trade of Under-Developed Countries', *Economic Bulletin for Latin America,* Vol. 8, pp. 1-7.

Kaldor, N. (1976) 'Inflation and Recession in the World Economy', *Economic Journal,* Vol. 86, pp. 703-14.

Kemp, M. C. (1955) 'Technological Change, the Terms of Trade and Welfare', *Economic Journal,* Vol. 65, pp. 457-73.

Kendrick, J. W. (1973) *Postwar Productivity Trends in the United States,* New York, National Bureau of Economic Research.

Kenwood, A. G. and Lougheed, A. L. (1971) *The Growth of the International Economy,* London, Allen & Unwin.

Keynes, J. M. (1920) *Economic Consequences of the Peace,* London, Macmillan.

Kindleberger, C. P. (1956) *The Terms of Trade: A European Case Study,* New York and London, Technology Press of MIT and John Wiley; and London, Chapman and Hall.

Kindleberger, C. P. (1958) 'The Terms of Trade and Economic Development', *Review of Economics and Statistics* (Supplement), Vol. 40 (Feb.), pp. 72–85.

Kojima, K. (1958) 'Japanese Foreign Trade and Economic Growth with Special Reference to the Terms of Trade', *Annals of Hitotsubashi Academy,* Vol. 8, pp. 143-68.

Kravis, I. B. and Lipsey, R. E. (1977) 'Export Prices and the Transmission of Inflation', *American Economic Review,* Vol. 67 (Feb.), pp. 155-63.

Kravis, I. B. and Lipsey, R. E. (1978) 'Price Behaviour in the Light of Balance of Payments Theories', *Journal of International Economics,* Vol. 8, pp. 193-246.

Kravis, I. B. and Lipsey, R. E. (1981) 'Prices and Terms of Trade for Developed Country Exports of Manufactures Goods', paper presented to the conference of the International Economic Association in Athens, 31 August–5 September 1981.

Krug, C. A. and de Poerck, R. A. (1968) *World Coffee Survey,* Rome, Food and Agriculture Organisation.

Kruger, A. O. (1978) *Foreign Trade Regimes and Economic Development: Liberalization Attempts and Consequences,* Cambridge, Mass., Ballinger Publishing Company for National Bureau of Economic Research.

Labys, W. C. (1978) 'Bibliography of Commodity Models', in F. G. Adams and J. R. Behrman (eds), *Econometric Modelling of World Commodity Policy,* Lexington and Toronto, D. C. Heath.

Laszlo, E. *et al.* (1978) *The Objectives of the New International Economic Order,* New York, Pergamon Press.
League of Nations (1945) *Industrialisation and Foreign Trade,* Geneva.
Leontieff, W. (1953) 'Domestic Production and Foreign Trade: The American Capital Position Re-examined', *Proceedings of the American Philosophical Society,* Vol. 97, pp. 332–49.
Lerdau, E. (1962) 'Some Notes on the Terms of Trade and Economic Development', *Quarterly Journal of Economics,* Vol. 76, pp. 464–70
Lewis, W. A. (1952) 'World Production, Prices and Trade, 1870–1960', *Manchester School of Economic and Social Studies,* Vol. 21, pp. 139–91.
Lewis, W. A. (1953) 'Economic Development with Unlimited Supplies of Labour', *Manchester School of Economic and Social Studies,* Vol. 21, pp. 139–91.
Lewis, W. A. (1955), *The Theory of Economic Growth,* London, Allen & Unwin.
Lewis, W. A. (1965) 'Economic Development and World Trade', in E. A. G. Robinson (ed.), *Problems in Economic Development,* London, Macmillan, pp. 483–95.
Lewis, W. A. (1969) *Aspects of Tropical Trade 1883-1965,* (Wicksell Lectures 1969), Stockholm, Almqvist and Wiksell.
Lewis, W. A. (1972) 'Reflections on Unlimited Labour', in L. E. Di Marco (ed.), *International Economics and Development: Essays in Honor of Paul Prebisch,* New York and London, Academic Press, pp. 75–96.
Lipsey, R. E. (1963) *Price and Quantity Trends in the Foreign Trade of the United States,* Princeton, Princeton University Press for the National Bureau of Economic Research.
Lipton, M. (1977) *Why the Poor Stay Poor,* Canberra, Australian University Press; London, Temple Smith.
Little, I. M. D. and Mirrlees, J. A. (1969) *Social Cost Benefit Analysis; Manual of Industrial Project Analysis in Developing Countries,* Vol. II, Paris, OECD.
Little, I. M. D., Scitovsky, T., and Scott, M. (1970) *Industry and Trade in Some Developing Countries: A Comparative Study,* London, Oxford University Press for OECD.
Llewellyn, G. E. J. (1974) 'The Determinants of United Kingdom Import Prices', *Economic Journal,* Vol. 84, pp. 18–31.
MacBean, A. (1978) *A Positive Approach to the International Economic Order,* Part I, *Trade and Structural Adjustment,* British–North American Committee.
MacBean, A. and Balasubramanyam, V. N. (1978) *Meeting the Third*

World Challenge, 2nd edn, London, Macmillan for Trade Policy Research Centre.

MacLaren, D. (1977) 'A Critique of the Proposed Agricultural Commodity Trading Arrangements Following UNCTAD IV', *National Westminster Bank Quarterly Review* (May), pp. 45–54.

Maizels, A. (1963) *Industrial Growth and World Trade*, Cambridge, Cambridge University Press.

Maizels, A. (1976) 'A New International Strategy for Primary Commodities' in G. K. Helleiner (ed.), *A World Divided: The Less Developed Countries in the International Economy,* Cambridge, Cambridge University Press, pp. 31–51.

Maizels, A. (1981) 'Selected Issues in the Negotiation of International Commodity Agreements', *Trade and Development, An UNCTAD Review* No. 3, pp. 53–78.

Malthus, T. R. (1820) *Principles of Political Economy,* London, John Murray.

Martin, K. and Thackeray, F. G. (1948) 'The Terms of Trade of Selected Countries', *Bulletin of Oxford University Institute of Statistics,* Vol. 10, pp. 373–94.

Marx, K. (1844) *Economic and Philosophic Manuscripts of 1844,* edited by D. J. Stuick; London, Lawrence and Wishart, 1970.

Meier, G. M. (1958) 'International Trade and International Inequality', *Oxford Economic Papers,* Vol. 10, pp. 277–89.

Meier, G. M. (1963) *International Trade and Development,* New York and Evanston, Harper and Row.

Meier, G. M. and Baldwin, R. E. (1957) *Economic Development: Theory, History, Policy,* New York, John Wiley.

Michaely, M. (1977) 'Exports and Growth: an Empirical Investigation', *Journal of Development Economics*, Vol. 4, pp. 49–53.

Mill, J. S. (1896) *Principles of Political Economy,* London, Longmans; New York, Green; Bombay, People's edn (transcript of 6th edn).

Mitra, A. (1977) *Terms of Trade and Class Relations*, London, Frank Cass.

Morgan, T. (1959–60) 'The Long-Run Terms of Trade Between Agriculture and Manufacturing', *Economic Development and Cultural Change,* Vol. 8, pp. 1–23.

Morgan, T. (1963) 'Trends in Terms of Trade and Their Repercussions on Primary Producers', in R. Harrod and D. Hague (eds), *International Trade Theory in a Developing World,* London, Macmillan.

Myrdal, G. (1956a) *Development and Underdevelopment,* Cairo, National Bank of Egypt.

Myrdal, G. (1956b) *An International Economy,* New York, Harper and Row.

Myrdal, G. (1968) *Asian Drama,* New York, Twentieth Century Fund.

Myrdal, G. (1970) *The Challenge of World Poverty,* New York, Pantheon Books, Random House.

Nadiri, M. I. (1970) 'Some Approaches to the Theory and Measurement of Total Factor Productivity: A Survey', *Journal of Economic Literature,* Vol. 7, pp. 1137-77.

Nelson, R. R. (1981) 'Research on Productivity Growth and Productivity Differences: Dead Ends and New Departures', *Journal of Economic Literature,* Vol. 19, pp. 1029-64.

Nurkse, R. (1959) *Patterns of Trade and Development* (Wicksell Lectures 1959), Stockholm, Almqvist and Wiksell.

Ohlin, B. (1933) *Inter-regional and International Trade*, Cambridge, Mass., Harvard University Press.

Palma, G. (1978) 'Dependency: A Formal Theory of Underdevelopment or a Methodology for the Analysis of Concrete Situations of Underdevelopment?', *World Development,* Vol. 6, pp. 881-924.

Pincus, J. (1967) *Trade, Aid and Development,* New York, McGraw Hill.

Pindyck, R. (1978) 'Gains to Producers from Cartelisation of an Exhaustible Resource', *Review of Economics and Statistics,* Vol. 60, pp. 238-45.

Prebisch, R. (1950) 'The Economic Development of Latin America and Its Principal Problems', *Economic Bulletin for Latin America* Vol. 7 (1962), pp. 1-22 (first published as an independent booklet by UN ECLA in 1950).

Prebisch, R. (1951) 'The Spread of Technical Progress and the Terms of Trade', in UN, *Economic Survey of Latin America* (1949), New York, UN Department of Economic Affairs, pp. 46-61.

Prebisch, R. (1959) 'Commerical Policies in Underdeveloped Countries', *American Economic Review,* Vol. 49, pp. 251-73.

Prebisch, R. (1963) 'Development Problems of the Peripheral Countries and the Terms of Trade', in UN, *Towards a Dynamic Development Policy for Latin America,* New York, UN, Part C, Chapter 1.

Prebisch, R. (1964) *Towards a New Trade Policy for Development,* Report by the Secretary General of UNCTAD, New York, UN.

Prebisch, R. (1976) 'A Critique of Peripheral Capitalism', *CEPAL Review,* UN ECLA, Vol. 1, pp. 9-76.

Pryor, F. L. (1966) 'Economic Growth and the Terms of Trade', *Oxford Economic Papers,* Vol. 18, pp. 45-57.

Pyatt, G. (1971) 'Profit Maximisation and the Threat of New Entry', *Economic Journal,* Vol. 81, pp. 242-55.

Radetzki, M. (1976) 'The Potential for Monopolistic Commodity Pricing by Developing Countries', in G. K. Helleiner (ed.), *A World*

Divided: The Less Developed Countries in the International Economy, Cambridge, Cambridge University Press.

Ray, G. F. (1977) 'The Real Price of Primary Products', *National Institute Economic Review,* (Aug.), pp. 72–6.

Ricardo, D. (1821) *Principles of Political Economy and Taxation,* 3rd edn, Harmondsworth, Middlesex, Penguin Books (1971); first published 1821.

Robertson, D. H. (1915) *A Study of Industrial Fluctuations,* London, King.

Robertson, D. H. (1952) 'The Terms of Trade' in D. H. Robertson, *Utility and All That and Other Essays,* London, Allen & Unwin, pp. 174–81.

Robinson, E. A. G. (1954) 'The Changing Structure of the British Economy', *Economic Journal,* Vol. 64, pp. 443–61.

Robinson, J. (1979) *Aspects of Development and Underdevelopment,* Cambridge, Cambridge University Press.

Rodriguez, O. (1977) 'On the Conception of the Centre-Periphery System', *CEPAL Review,* UN ECLA, Vol. 3, pp. 195–239.

Samuelson, P. A. (1948) 'International Trade and the Equalisation of Factor Prices', *Economic Journal,* Vol. 58, pp. 163–84.

Samuelson, P. A. (1949) 'International Factor-Price Equalisation Once Again', *Economic Journal,* Vol. 59, pp. 181–97.

Samuelson, P. A. (1971) 'Ohlin Was Right', *Swedish Journal of Economics,* Vol. 73, pp. 365–84.

Sau, R. (1978) *Unequal Exchange, Imperialism and Underdevelopment,* Calcutta, Oxford University Press.

Schloss, H. H. (1977) 'Declining Terms of Trade: Myth or Reality', *Economia Internazionale,* Vol. 30, pp. 466–9.

Schlote, W. (1952) *British Overseas Trade from 1700 to the 1930s,* Oxford, Blackwell, first published in German in 1938.

Sid-Ahmed, A. (1981) *Nord-Sud: Les Enjeux (Théorie et Pratique du Nouvel Ordre Economique International),* Paris, Eds Publisud.

Singer, H. (1950) 'The Distribution of Gains between Investing and Borrowing Countries', *American Economic Review,* Vol. 40 (May), pp. 473–85.

Singer, H. (1958) 'Comment' on Kindleberger's 'The Terms of Trade and Economic Development', *Review of Economics and Statistics* (Supplement), Vol. 40 (Feb. 1958), pp. 85–8.

Singer, H. (1974–5) 'The Distribution of Gains from Trade and Investment Revisited', *Journal of Development Studies,* Vol. 11, pp. 376–82.

Spence, A. M. (1977) 'Entry Capacity, Investment and Oligopolistic Pricing', *Bell Journal of Economics,* Vol. 8, pp. 534–44.

Spence, A. M. (1979) 'Investment Strategy and Growth in a New Market', *Bell Journal of Economics,* Vol. 10, pp. 1-19.

Spraos, J. (1977) 'Why Inflation is not Relative Price-Neutral for Primary Products', *World Development,* Vol. 5, pp. 707-13.

Spraos, J. (1979) 'The Theory of Deteriorating Terms of Trade Revisited', *Greek Economic Review,* Vol. 1 (Dec.) pp. 15-42.

Spraos, J. (1980) 'The Statistical Debate on the Net Barter Terms of Trade Between Primary Products and Manufactures', *Economic Journal,* Vol. 90, pp. 107-28.

Staehle, H. (1951) 'Some Notes on the Terms of Trade', *International Social Science Bulletin,* Vol. 3, pp. 33-7.

Streeten, P. (1974) 'World Trade in Agricultural Commodities and the Terms of Trade with Industrial Goods', in N. Islam (ed.), *Agricultural Policy in Developing Countries,* London, Macmillan, pp. 207-23.

Streeten, P. (1982) 'Approaches to a New International Economic Order', *World Development,* Vol. 10, pp. 1-17.

Sylos-Labini, P. (1982) 'Rigid Prices, Flexible Prices and Inflation', *Banca Nazionale del Lavoro Quarterly Review,* Vol. 35, pp. 37-68.

Torrens, R. (1829) *An Essay on the External Corn Trade,* London; Longman, Rees, Orme, Brown, and Green, 5th edn.

United Nations (1949) *Relative Prices of Exports and Imports of Underdeveloped Countries,* Lake Success, New York, UN.

United Nations, *Statistical Yearbook.*

UNCTAD, *Handbook of International Trade and Development Statistics.*

United Nations Economic and Social Council (1975) *Measurement of Price Changes in External Trade,* CES/AC, 45/2 (14 March).

United Nations Economic Commission for Europe (1968) *The World Market for Iron Ore,* New York.

United States Department of Agriculture (1971) *Cotton in Greece,* (Dec.) Foreign Agricultural Service.

United States Department of Commerce, and Bureau of the Census and Statistics Canada (1970) *The Reconciliation of US-Canada Trade Statistics.*

Van Meerhaeghe, M A. G. (1969) 'Observations sur la Signification des Termes d'Echange des Pays Sous-développés', *Kyklos*, Vol. 22, pp. 566-84.

Viner, J. (1937) *Studies in the Theory of International Trade,* London, Allen & Unwin.

Viner, J. (1953) *International Trade and Economic Development,* Oxford, Clarendon Press.

Vining, D. R. and Elbertowski, T. C. (1976) 'The Relationship Between

Relative Prices and the General Price Level', *American Economic Review,* Vol. 66, pp. 699–708.

Wenders, J. T. (1971-2) 'Excess Capacity as a Barrier to Entry', *Journal of Industrial Economics,* Vol. 20, pp. 14–19.

Wilson T. *et al.* (1969) 'The Income Terms of Trade of Developed and Developing Countries', *Economic Journal,* Vol. 79, pp. 813–32.

World Bank (1975) *Price Forecasts for Major Primary Commodities,* Report No. 814, Washington DC.

World Bank (1976, 1978, 1980) *Price Prospects for Major Primary Commodities,* Report Nos 814/1976, 814/1978, 814/1980, Washington DC.

World Bank (1980) *Methodologies for Measuring Agricultural Price Intervention Effects,* Staff Working Paper No. 394, Washington DC.

Yates, P. L. (1959) *Forty Years of Foreign Trade,* London, Allen & Unwin.

Yeats, A. J. (1981) *Trade and Development: Leading issues for the 1980s,* London and Basingstoke, Macmillan.

INDEX